The Usborne
Big Book
of
Picture Puzzles

Jane Bingham, Rosie Heywood
and Kamini Khanduri

Illustrated by
Dominic Groebner, David Hancock, Inklink Firenze
and Studio Gallante

Contents

THE GREAT
HISTORY
SEARCH

Illustrated by David Hancock

In the town on pages 34 and 35, some poor people lived in a workhouse.

On the American prairies on pages 36 and 37, many people rode in wagons.

Electric stoves were on sale in the department store on pages 38 and 39.

Turn to pages 32 and 33 to see all the people at the French ball in their best clothes.

You'll find this painting of a Dutch family on pages 30 and 31.

The Indian emperor on pages 28 and 29 sat on this beautiful throne.

The palace gardens were lit by paper lanterns at the Chinese party on pages 26 and 27.

Contents

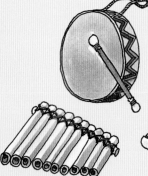
The Incas on pages 24 and 25 played all kinds of musical instruments.

Jesters lived in medieval castles. See who else lived there on pages 22 and 23.

There was a dancing bear at the village fair on pages 20 and 21.

About the puzzles

Early people painted pictures on their cave walls. See how they lived on pages 4 and 5.

In this part of the book, you can find out about different people and places from history. But this isn't just a history book, it's a puzzle book, too. This shows how the puzzles work and gives a few tips to help you solve them.

The farmers on pages 6 and 7 used tools like this sickle.

This strip tells you the date and sometimes the place. BC is before Christ and AD is after Christ.

Around the edge of the big picture, there are lots of little pictures.

The writing next to each little picture tells you how many of that thing you can find in the big picture.

This wagon in the distance counts.

Prairie homes

People wrote on clay tablets in the Mesopotamian city on pages 8 and 9.

Find out how the Egyptians built pyramids on pages 10 and 11.

Part of this wall has been taken away, so you can see inside.

You can only see part of this gun, but it still counts.

This cowboy coming out of the big picture counts as a little picture too.

The puzzle is to find the people, objects and animals in each big picture. Some are easy to spot, but some are tiny, or hidden behind other things. If the big picture is in two halves (pages 4–5 and 12–13), you have to look in both halves. You'll find all the answers on pages 40–45.

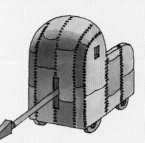

The Assyrians used siege engines in the battle on pages 12 and 13.

Find out what the Vikings hung on their walls on pages 18 and 19.

Turn to pages 16 and 17 to find out why Romans took a flask of oil to the bath house.

People at the Greek market on pages 14 and 15 paid with coins like this one.

Early people

People shot animals with bows and arrows. Spot a boy who has shot a bird.

The old people told the children exciting stories. Can you find two storytellers?

Fish caught from the river were hung to dry on wooden frames. Spot 20.

Axes were stones on wooden handles. Find two.

People used these digging sticks to dig for roots in the ground. Spot three.

Baskets were woven from rushes. Find nine.

People made tools from flints. Spot four other people chipping away at flints.

Early people moved around with the seasons, hunting animals and gathering plants to eat. The left-hand page shows some early people in Europe, spending the winter in a cave. The right-hand page shows them in summer.

People painted animal pictures on the cave walls. Spot three deer pictures.

Lamps were made by burning fur soaked in animal fat. Find five.

Women gathered berries in leather bags. Find three bags.

Men went hunting for wild animals. Find seven wild deer.

Skins and furs were sewn into coverings and clothes. Find five people sewing.

Babies were wrapped up warmly. Spot nine.

People scraped skins to clean them. Spot four skins being scraped.

Paint was made from soft rocks and animal fat. Find three people making paint.

People hung skins to dry on wooden racks. Spot five.

Antler

Some tools were made from antlers. Can you find four people carving antlers?

Necklaces were made from shells, stones, bones or teeth. Find 12.

People wore furs in winter and skins in summer. Spot a child being dressed.

Wooden spears with sharp flint tips were used for hunting. Spot 11.

Meat was roasted over a fire. Spot six people cooking.

5

Flat loaves of bread were baked on clay ovens. Can you spot eight ovens?

Wooden ladders were used for building. Find three.

Women fetched water from the stream. Find seven women with water pots on their heads.

Spot three cooking pots.

Fish were caught in the stream. Spot four people fishing with nets.

People rolled out pieces of clay to make pots. Find two people making pots.

First farmers

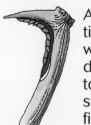

At harvest time, crops were cut down with tools called sickles. Spot five sickles.

Farming began when people learned to plant seeds and grow crops. They also tamed animals. These changes meant people could stay in one place instead of moving around. This is a farming village in the Middle East.

Men went hunting for wild animals. Spot two men coming back from a hunting trip.

Women made thread by spinning wool around a spindle. Spot three spindles.

The chief offered gifts to a statue of the village goddess. Find the statue.

6

Thatched roofs on houses caught fire easily. Find a fire on a roof.

The grain from the crop was put into big baskets. Spot seven baskets.

Find two men mending the mud-brick wall around the village.

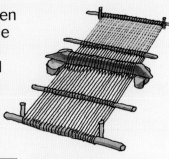

Thread was woven into cloth on a wooden frame called a loom. Spot three.

Sheep were kept for wool, milk and meat. Find 20.

Goats were kept for milk, skins and meat. Find four.

Pigs were kept for meat. Find six pigs and six piglets.

Cattle were kept for milk, skins and meat. Find 16.

Geese were kept for feathers, eggs and meat. Can you spot 11?

Children helped look after herds of animals. Find four herders with sticks.

Stones were used to grind grain into flour. Spot four women grinding.

Dogs helped with hunting and herding other animals. Spot eight.

Children scared birds away from the crops. Find four children scaring birds.

7

Living in cities

Furniture was made of wood. Spot five chairs.

Most people couldn't read or write, so they hired scribes. Spot one scribe.

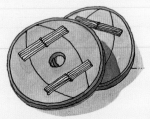

Wheels were made from three pieces of wood joined together. Can you spot ten?

Soldiers wore long cloaks and helmets, and carried spears. Find 16.

Baskets were used for fruit, vegetables and grain. Spot 14.

People used metal tubes as drinking straws. Spot four people using straws.

Early cities had temples, schools and lots of houses. This city is in Mesopotamia. The temple is on a big stepped platform, called a ziggurat. People are going there in a procession, to offer gifts to the city's god.

Buildings had flat roofs. Spot 40 people on rooftops.

Merchants used donkeys to carry packs. Spot four with packs.

Rich boys went to school. Schools were very strict. Spot a schoolboy sneaking in late.

Find four people playing harps like this one.

Spot two pairs of men playing this game.

Dresses were fastened at the shoulder. Find nine women in blue dresses.

People wrote on clay tablets. Spot someone running with a message on a tablet.

Find three metalsmiths who are pouring hot metal into hollow clay shapes.

The king ruled the city. Can you see him in his chariot with the queen?

Potters made clay pots on a wheel. Spot four potter's wheels.

Jars were used to carry wine. Find someone who has broken a jar.

People used seals to sign things. The picture on the seal was rolled into soft clay. Spot one seal.

Stone seal

Rolling the seal

Picture on clay

Can you see a farmer bringing some sheep as a payment to the king?

9

Pyramids

A ramp of rubble was built to reach the upper levels. Spot someone falling off the ramp.

The king and some other rich people kept pets. Find five dogs.

Grit 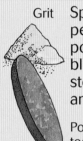 Spot four people polishing blocks with stone tools and grit.

Polishing tool

The architect planned the building. Can you see him looking at his plans?

Here's the doctor's tool basket. Find the doctor.

The queen had a pet monkey. Spot the monkey being naughty.

Ancient Egyptian kings and queens were buried inside big stone pyramids, which were built while they were still alive. There were no machines, so a pyramid took about 20 years to build. This one is in its early stages.

This is what the finished pyramid looked like. Find two models of finished pyramids.

Mallet

Chisel

Stonemasons used chisels to chip off rough edges. Can you find six?

The king came to check on the work. Can you see him being carried in his chair?

Find eight men using wooden poles to lever stone blocks into place.

Teams of men pulled the blocks along on sleds. Find nine sleds.

Carpenters used hammers to mend broken sleds. Spot six hammers.

Measuring instruments were used to check each block was level. Find five.

The queen would have her own pyramid beside the king's. Spot the queen.

Oil was used to help the sleds move smoothly. Spot four jars of oil.

The overseer was in charge of the building work. Can you see him pointing angrily with his stick?

Baskets were used for carrying rubble. Find a man with a hole in his basket.

Birds called hawks looked for food around the building site. Find seven.

Metalsmiths made and mended tools. Spot three saws like this one.

Scribes made lists of how many blocks and tools were being used. Spot six scribes.

Going into battle

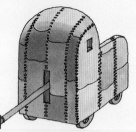

Battering ram

Siege engines with battering rams inside were used to break through the city walls. Spot five siege engines.

Can you find four horses swimming across the river?

Archers attacked with bows and arrows. Spot 12 bows.

Soldiers wore tunics, leggings and boots. Spot four soldiers putting on their boots.

Spot five soldiers carrying sacks full of stolen goods.

Some soldiers attacked with swords. Find 15 swords.

The Assyrian people had a big army of soldiers. The top part of this picture shows the soldiers marching into battle.

The bottom part shows them attacking a city. They stole things and captured people from the places they attacked.

Many people were captured by the soldiers. Spot seven captives with their hands tied.

Some horses wore bright saddle cloths. Spot four yellow cloths.

There was fighting on top of the walls. Spot seven people falling.

12

The soldiers stole animals. Spot seven sheep being led away.

Even children were captured. Find a mother comforting a child with a drink.

The soldiers carried shields. Spot someone who has dropped his shield.

Inflated skins were used as floats to cross rivers. Spot someone who has let go of his float.

The king rode into battle in his chariot. Can you see him?

Soldiers used ladders made of wood. Can you find eight?

Many soldiers attacked with spears. Spot a broken spear.

Slingers attacked by hurling big stones from leather slings. Can you spot seven others?

Small boats were used to carry things across rivers. Spot four boats.

Scribes made lists of how many people had been killed or captured. Find two scribes.

Soldiers on horseback were called the cavalry. Spot two soldiers on white horses.

At the market

The barber cut people's hair. Find a man who hates his new haircut.

This coin is from Athens. Other cities had their own coins. Spot a man dropping all his money.

Officials checked the weight of things. Find six sets of weighing scales.

People ate olives and used olive oil for cooking and in lamps. Spot someone eating olives.

Can you find four dogs?

Rich people shopped with their slaves. Spot a slave with too much shopping.

This picture shows a busy marketplace in the city of Athens in Greece. A Greek marketplace was called an agora. All the shops were under a covered area called a stoa. Out in the open, there were lots of stalls.

Soldiers had spears and big bronze helmets. Can you see five soldiers?

Cats were rare pets for rich people. Find four cats which have escaped.

Fish was a very popular food. Spot four people who have been to a fish stall.

Find three children playing with hoops.

The wine-seller let some people taste his wine. Spot four people drinking wine.

Can you find three people carrying the sandals they have bought?

Wise men called philosophers met to discuss science and politics. Spot two arguing.

There were often statues of gods or famous people. Find two statues.

Lamps were the only lighting used in houses. Find the lamp stall.

People from outside the city had to change money at the banker's stall. Spot the banker.

Rich people bought slaves. Spot a slave who is trying to escape from his new master.

Some people wore hats when it was sunny. Find five hats.

Pottery was often beautifully painted. Spot five two-handled jars like this.

Actors in plays wore masks like this. Find three actors going to a rehearsal.

The bath house

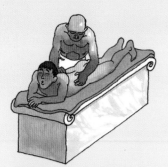

To relax, people had their bodies massaged by a slave. Spot four people having a massage.

Lots of exercises went on at the baths. Find five people lifting weights.

Spot someone stealing another man's clothes from a changing room locker.

The hot room was called the caldarium. Can you find it?

The Romans made lots of statues. Can you find a statue of the emperor?

People used sticks called strigils to scrape oil and dirt off their bodies. Spot five.

Roman towns had public bath houses, with hot, warm and cold baths. People went to bathe, but also to talk about business, to exercise, or just to gossip. A visit might last hours, and lots of people went every day.

Fighting men called gladiators were very popular. Spot this gladiator with all his fans.

Women went to a separate bath house. Find five women with their towels.

People wore sandals in the hot room, so as not to burn their feet. Spot a man who has forgotten his sandals.

16

Apartments near the baths were noisy. Find a man who is complaining about the noise.

Instead of soap, people used oil to clean their bodies. Spot 11 oil flasks.

Find eight soldiers with their helmets.

Some floors were covered with mosaics (pictures made from pieces of stone). Spot a mosaic floor.

Attendants worked at the baths. Find an attendant with a pile of towels.

Food, such as pastries and olives, was on sale. Spot two trays of food.

The cold room was called the frigidarium. Can you see where it is?

Can you see someone putting on a toga — a very big piece of material?

People paid to enter the baths. Spot a thief who has run off with someone's purse.

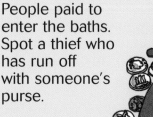

Most large bath houses had a library, with scrolls to read. Find the library.

Scroll

Water was heated by a boiler over a fire. Spot a slave who has fainted from the heat.

Boiler

17

Winter feasts

Cloth was woven on a big loom. Can you see the loom?

Women fastened their tunics with brooches. Find someone doing up her brooch.

Firewood was kept outside. Spot two people gathering wood.

There were spoons and knives, but no forks. Find 12 spoons.

Women wore dresses with tunics on top. Spot someone with a torn tunic.

A poet called a skald played the harp and recited poems. Find the poet.

The Vikings lived in northern Europe. The men were fierce warriors who sailed abroad in their big ships. At home, most Vikings lived in long houses, in small villages. Here, a village chief is giving a feast in his house.

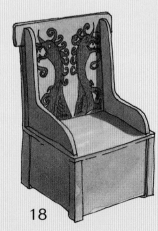

The chief had his own chair. Can you find him?

Wool tapestries hung on the walls. Find a child hiding behind one.

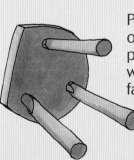

People sat on stools or on wooden platforms along the walls. Spot someone falling off a stool.

When they were not being used, weapons were often hung on the walls. Find five swords.

Beer, wine and mead (a honey drink) were poured from jugs. Spot six.

Acrobats entertained the guests. Find a pair of acrobats.

Food was cooked over an open fire. Spot someone stirring a cauldron full of stew.

The chief had his own servants. Spot a servant with a pile of bowls.

Oil lamps in tall metal holders lit the house. Find five.

People drank from animal horns or wooden cups. Spot 12 drinking horns.

Vegetables and dried fish were hung from the rafters. Spot ten dried fish.

Wine, beer and salted food were stored in wooden barrels. Spot seven.

Men kept hunting dogs. Can you see two fighting?

Clothes and valuable things were kept in chests. Find an open chest.

19

Village life

Can you see someone using stepping stones to cross the stream?

Merchants came to the fair from nearby towns. Spot a merchant unloading wine from a cart.

Hoe

Houses had vegetable plots. Spot someone using each of these tools.

Rake

Spade

Things for sale at the fair were put on tables. Spot four.

There was lots to see at the fair. Find a dancing bear.

Stocks

People who did wrong were punished. Spot a man with his legs in the stocks.

In the Middle Ages, most of the people in Europe lived in small villages. A few villagers owned their own land. The rest lived and worked on land owned by a lord. In this English village, the summer fair is being set up.

The lord lived in a big house or a castle. Can you see him setting off on a hunting trip?

People went to church often. Spot the priest sweeping the church porch.

People wore different kinds of hats. Spot ten pointed hoods.

The blacksmith made and mended metal tools. Can you find him?

Can you see three people chopping firewood outside their houses?

Milk was made into butter in a churn. Spot two churns.

Everyone had their grain ground into flour at the village windmill. Can you see it?

People kept bees for honey. Spot a man being chased by a swarm of bees.

Chickens were kept for meat, feathers and eggs. Spot two people feeding chickens.

Find the miller taking money for grinding some grain.

Can you spot someone going around selling small things from a tray?

Lots of things were bought and sold at the fair. Spot a big pile of cheeses.

Cats were useful for catching rats and mice. Find nine other cats.

Most people had fleas and head lice. Find a woman picking lice from her child's hair.

21

Castle life

In the Middle Ages, kings and lords in Europe built huge stone castles. Armies of fierce soldiers guarded them. The strong, stone walls kept enemies out, but castles were often cold, damp places to live in.

The jester's job was to make people laugh. Spot the jester.

Spot 20 guards on the battlements, looking out for enemies.

The waste from toilets dropped down to the ground below. Can you find two toilets?

Prisoners were kept in the dungeon. Spot a prisoner in chains.

Servants were always busy. Spot a servant with a tray of goblets.

There was enough food stored to last months. Spot the storeroom.

The lord and his wife slept in a big bed with curtains all around it. Find the bed.

This is the lord. Can you see him in his office counting out his money?

Fierce birds called falcons were trained to hunt. Find three.

People didn't wash often. Spot someone in a bathtub.

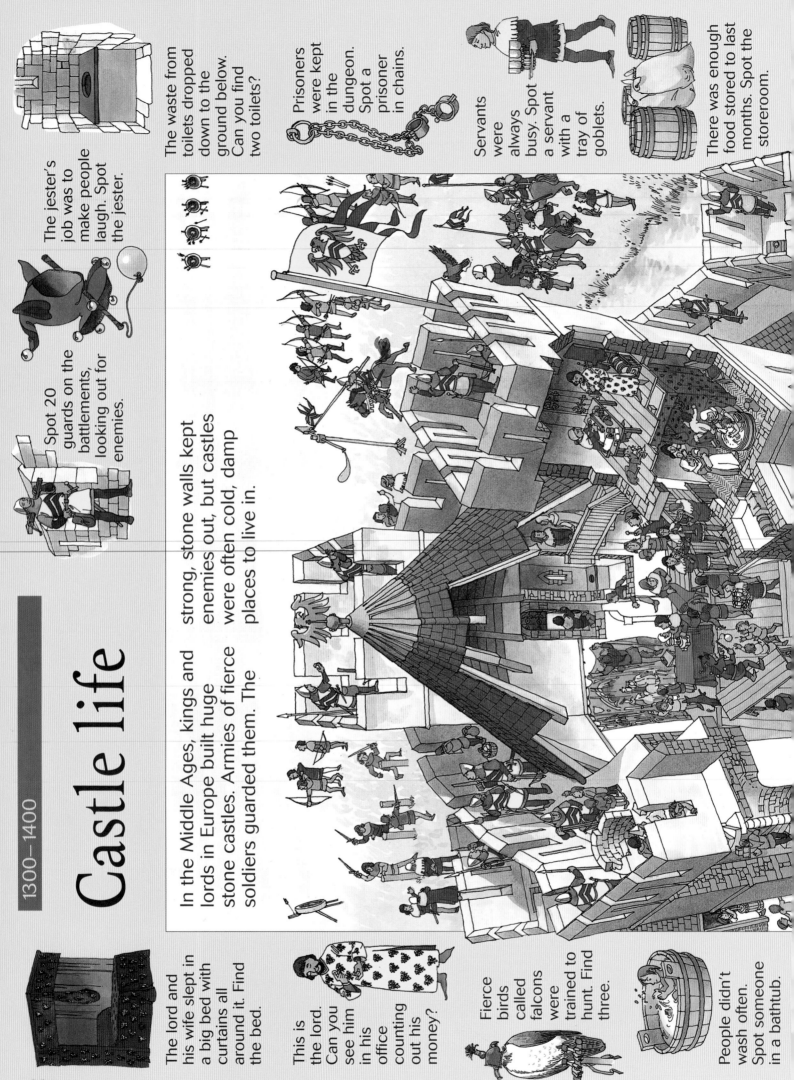

22

Knights on horseback trained to fight with long spears called lances. Find four.

Tapestries helped keep out the cold. Spot someone hanging a tapestry.

Musicians called minstrels played from a gallery. Can you see them?

The castle had stone spiral staircases. Spot someone falling down the stairs.

Windows had shutters on the inside. Spot someone looking out of a window.

Find ten archers at shooting practice with their bows and arrows.

Water was pulled up in buckets from a well. Spot the well.

Find three horses looking out of their stables.

Guards who were off duty rested in the guardroom. Find the guardroom.

Everyone had a job to do. Can you see the candle-maker?

The priest held religious services in the chapel. Can you find it?

23

Inca homes

Buildings were made from stone blocks which fitted together perfectly. Spot four storehouses.

The soft wool from alpacas was used to make clothes. Find eight.

Bridges were made out of reeds. Spot two.

Women often carried babies on their backs. Find eight babies.

Knotted strings, called quipus, were used to store information. Spot four.

Guinea pigs were not pets, but were kept for meat. Can you find 12?

The Incas lived in the Andes mountains of South America. They built cities and strong stone roads. In this farming village, people are growing crops of corn and potatoes on terraces (steps of land dug into the mountainside).

Llamas were used to carry packs. Find a llama sitting down.

Messengers called chasquis ran quickly to deliver messages. Spot four.

Trumpets called pototos were made from shells. The sound carried far. Find one.

Looms had a strap, which went around the weaver's back. Spot three.

Sandal soles were made of llama skin. Find someone putting on some sandals.

This big mountain bird is a condor. Spot another one.

Spot someone making a drink called chicha by spitting chewed fruit into water.

Potatoes grew well on the high slopes. Find ten sacks of potatoes.

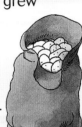

Wooden sticks like this were used for digging. Find ten digging sticks.

Women made flour by grinding corn between stones. Spot a woman grinding.

Cooking pots were all shapes and sizes. Find one like this.

Children scared birds away from the crops by firing stones from slings. Find two slings.

Musical instruments were played on special occasions. Spot each of these.

Panpipes

Drum

Flute

The Inca emperor was a strict ruler. Can you see him in his litter, coming to inspect the village?

Litter

A Chinese party

People used fans to keep cool. Spot three fans.

Pottery, clothes and furniture were often decorated with dragon pictures. Find eight.

Silk covers were draped over chairs. Find four chair covers.

People ate rice with almost every meal. Find a half-finished bowl of rice.

Incense burner

People burned incense to make a sweet smell. Spot an incense burner.

Many people kept pet dogs. Find seven.

Chinese emperors and noblemen lived in beautiful palaces with lovely gardens. Most other people in China were poor. In this picture, a rich nobleman is having a firework party. He is sitting on the veranda with his wife.

Wood was often covered with a shiny substance called lacquer. Find seven lacquered trays.

Find the palace gardener and his children watching the fireworks.

Gong

Drum

Flute

Musicians entertained the guests. Spot these musical instruments.

Men and women wore silk robes. Find eight red robes.

Fireworks were invented in China. Spot a servant lighting a firework.

Paintings on silk or paper scrolls were hung on walls. Find two.

Officials took notes at important events. Find an official with his boy assistant.

Rich people had statues in their gardens. Find two statues like this.

People poured tea from teapots and drank it from little bowls. Spot four teapots.

Lanterns were made of paper and had candles inside. Spot ten.

People used chopsticks to eat their food. Spot six pairs of chopsticks.

People went to temples but they also had shrines at home for worship. Find one.

Shrine

A type of pottery called porcelain was invented in China. Spot six jars like this one.

Screens were used as doors, or for decoration. They were often painted. Find one.

Indian wedding

Some people rode on elephants, on seats called howdahs. Find five elephants.

The holy man blessed the bride and groom. Can you see him?

Weavers made beautiful things. Find these three woven things.

Red and gold wall hanging

Black and white cushion

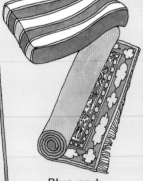

Blue and green carpet

The palace had lovely gardens. Can you spot a gardener with a spade?

Can you see someone wearing this jewel in his turban?

The Mogul emperors in India were very rich. They lived in grand palaces like this one. Here, everyone is celebrating because the emperor's son is getting married. They are watching the wedding procession.

The emperor's golden throne was decorated with diamonds and rubies. Find it.

People wore gowns called jamas and trousers called piajamas. Spot a man in these clothes.

Yellow jama

Striped piajamas

Men wore turbans on their heads. Spot ten dark blue turbans.

Silver bowl

Emerald necklace

Wood and ivory box

Jade wine cup

Mogul craftsmen made lots of beautiful things. Find each of these.

The palace artist painted pictures of important events. Can you find him?

The Moguls had many weapons. Spot a dagger with a horse's head on it.

People smoked pipes called hookahs. Find a man smoking.

Spot the musicians playing these instruments.

Brass trumpet

Drum

Sitar

Tambourine

The bride and groom would not have met before the wedding. Find them.

Groom

Bride

The emperor kept birds at the palace. Find six peacocks.

Most people in India were very poor. Spot this group of beggars outside the palace.

29

Busy ports

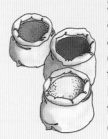

Sailors used astrolabes on voyages, to measure the height of stars. Can you see one?

There were lots of jobs to be done, even in port. Find these workers.

Rope-fitter

Sail mender

Carpenter

Most houses were tall and narrow, with a top part called a gable. Spot a green gable.

Goods were pulled up to storerooms in attics by machines called winches. Find three.

In the 1600s, Holland was a very rich country. Big ships, owned by merchants, sailed abroad to buy and sell goods. This is a busy Dutch port. A big ship has just arrived home from a long voyage and is being unloaded.

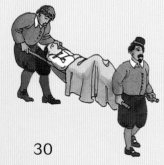

On long voyages, fresh food ran out, so many sailors became ill or died. Spot a sick sailor.

As well as roads, many Dutch towns had canals. Find an open bridge over a canal.

Tulips were rare and expensive. Can you see some?

Artists painted pictures of merchants and their families. Spot an artist.

Ships had guns in case they were attacked by enemies. Find four guns.

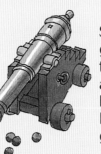

The ship owner paid the crew after each voyage. Find him.

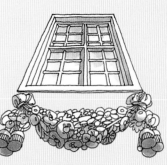

Many houses had stone fruit garlands, called swags, under their windows.

Sailors were often injured on voyages. Spot a sailor who has a wooden leg.

People played musical instruments at home. Find this virginal.

Rich people had servants. Spot the servants who are doing these jobs.

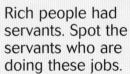

Hanging up laundry

Scrubbing floor tiles

Polishing silver

The telescope was invented in Holland. Spot a scientist using his telescope.

Many goods, such as tea and sugar, came from China, India or Africa. Find these things.

Porcelain

Silk

Ivory

Some rich people ran homes for orphans. Find two ladies collecting a homeless child.

31

At the ball

There were lots of clocks at the palace. Find two.

Men wore wigs made of goat, horse or human hair. Can you see someone whose wig has fallen off?

Both men and women made up their faces. Spot someone checking his face in a pocket mirror.

Shoes often had fine embroidery and buckles. Find these shoes.

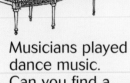

Musicians played dance music. Can you find a harpsichord?

Women curtsied and men bowed to the King. Spot the King.

Jar of smelling salts

The French King Louis XV lived in a fine palace at Versailles, near Paris. He entertained lots of rich people there. In this picture, everyone is at a ball, in a beautiful long room called the Hall of Mirrors.

Women often fainted from the heat. Spot a maid bringing smelling salts to revive her mistress.

The Hall of Mirrors had 17 arched mirrors. Find five of them.

Most people knew the steps for many different dances. Spot a dancer who has fallen over.

The King had hundreds of servants. Can you spot a servant pouring wine?

Dresses had very wide skirts. Find eight pink dresses with this pattern.

Men wore jackets, short trousers called breeches, and silk stockings. Spot a man in these clothes.

Women wore decorations in their hair. Find 11 wearing flowers in their hair.

Women stuck beauty spots on their faces. Find four women with beauty spots.

Hanging glass holders called chandeliers held candles. Can you find four others?

The palace was full of beautiful, expensive furniture. Can you see a couch?

Oranges

Salmon

Chicken

All kinds of tasty food was served at the ball. Spot these dishes.

People drank from crystal glasses. Can you spot someone spilling her wine?

Women carried pretty, painted fans. Find 11 women peeping over their fans.

There were rules about how to behave in front of the King. Spot someone who has misbehaved.

Factory town

Richer people used carriages called hansom cabs as taxis. Find two.

Boats called barges were used to transport heavy goods on canals. Spot three.

People fetched water from pumps in the street. Spot someone pumping water.

Spot the people selling these things from carts or barrows.

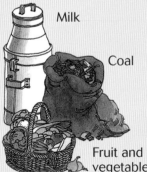

Milk

Coal

Fruit and vegetables

Children worked in mines, factories or on the streets. Spot a child selling matches.

Tray of matches

This is a town in England. When big machines for making cloth and other things were invented, many country people moved to towns like this, to work in factories. The streets were noisy, crowded and dirty.

Homeless children and old people were sent to a harsh place called a workhouse. Can you find one?

Steam trains carried passengers and goods all over the country at low cost. Spot a train.

Coal was the main fuel, so lots of people worked down coal mines. Spot six miners with lamps.

Miner's lamp

Sweep's brush

Chimney sweeps climbed up dark, sooty chimneys. Spot three sweeps.

Barber's

Shoemaker's

Tailor's

People bought things from small shops. Find these shops.

Streets were lit by gas lamps. Can you spot ten?

In factories, people worked long hours. Can you spot a tired worker who has fallen asleep?

Newspapers were on sale for people who could read. Spot a paper-seller.

The police tried to stop people from causing trouble or committing crimes. Spot six policemen.

Spot the people doing these jobs on the streets.

Selling pies

Lighting lamps

Selling flowers

Some orphans lived on the streets, stealing money or begging. Spot these beggars.

The filthy streets and houses were full of rats. Spot the rat-catcher doing his rounds.

The barrel organ player entertained people in the street. Can you see him?

Barrel organ

35

Prairie homes

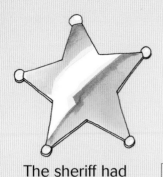

The blacksmith made horseshoes. Can you find him?

The sheriff had to keep law and order. He wore a star-shaped badge. Find him.

People who lived outside town came in to buy things. Spot someone buying this lamp.

There was only one school in town, with one teacher. Find the teacher.

Most people went to church on Sundays. Can you see the church?

There were no phones, but people sent messages by telegraph. Spot six telegraph poles.

For many years, the plains, or prairies, of North America were home to Native Americans. Then, settlers from the East took over the land, and built towns and railways. In this town, people are preparing for a holiday.

Some people kept on moving West. Spot a family loading their wagon.

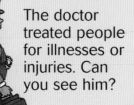

The doctor treated people for illnesses or injuries. Can you see him?

Trains carried people, goods and cattle to other towns and cities. Find where the train stops.

Sometimes, robbers tried to steal money from the bank. Spot two.

Most men had guns. Can you find eight guns?

Handgun
Rifle

Men drank and played cards in a bar called a saloon. Spot the barman.

Wagons were used to carry heavy loads. Spot three with covers and three without.

People entertained each other with music. Find these instruments.

Accordion

Piano

Guitar

Some Native Americans lived near the town in areas called reservations. Spot four.

Many people worked on the railways. Spot five men laying new tracks.

LAUNDRY

RESTAURANT

CORRAL

DEPOT

Cowboys brought cattle into town. Spot eight other cowboys.

Richer people owned small carriages called buggies. Can you find two?

The local newspaper was printed once a week. Spot the newspaper office.

Printing press

37

Department stores

When the first department stores opened, people could buy all kinds of things in one building, instead of going to lots of shops.

Spot a fashion show going on in the women's clothes department.

Paperback books didn't cost much. Spot someone buying this book.

All kinds of toys were sold in the toy department. Spot six of each of these.

Teddy bear

Grey rocking horse

Red pedal car

Can you see where people are buying baby clothes?

People played records on a phonograph. Spot someone choosing one.

The store had its own letter box where mail was collected. Find it.

Jars of orange bonbons

Chocolates on stands

Tins of toffees

Spot these things in the confectionery department.

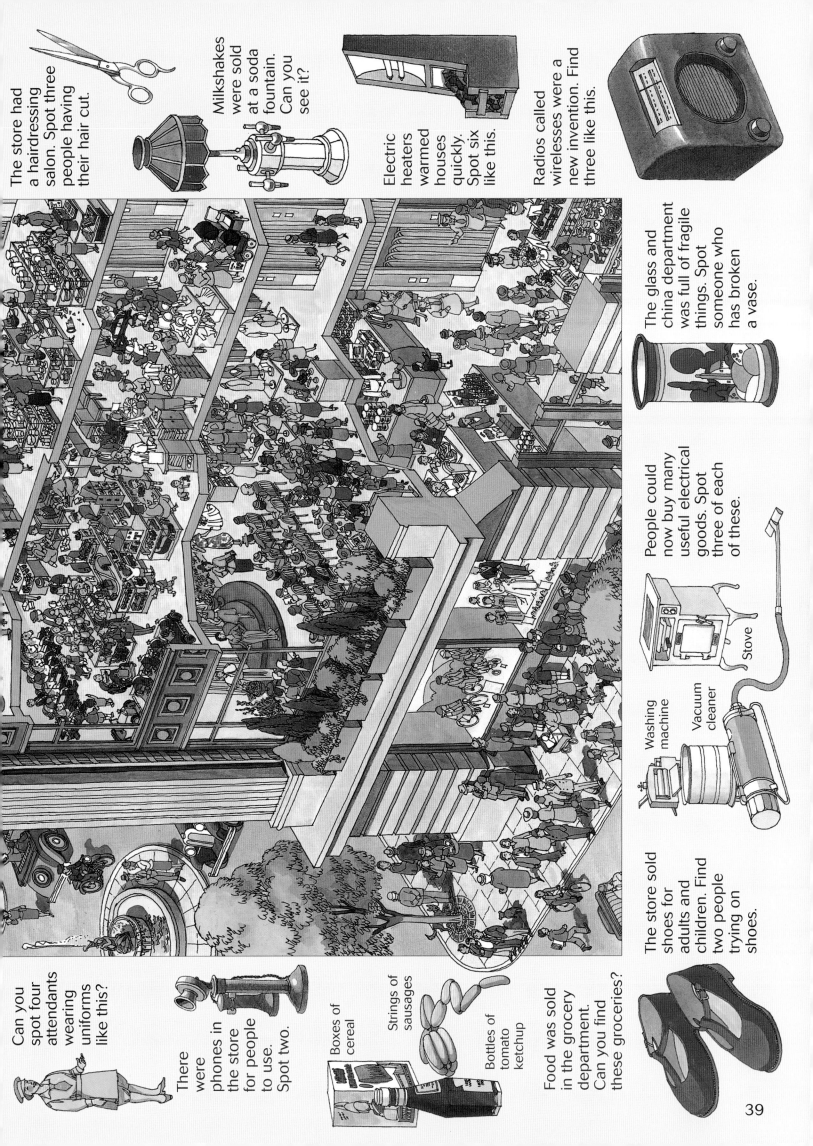

The store had a hairdressing salon. Spot three people having their hair cut.

Milkshakes were sold at a soda fountain. Can you see it?

Electric heaters warmed houses quickly. Spot six like this.

Radios called wirelesses were a new invention. Find three like this.

The glass and china department was full of fragile things. Spot someone who has broken a vase.

People could now buy many useful electrical goods. Spot three of each of these.

Washing machine

Vacuum cleaner

Stove

The store sold shoes for adults and children. Find two people trying on shoes.

Can you spot four attendants wearing uniforms like this?

There were phones in the store for people to use. Spot two.

Boxes of cereal

Strings of sausages

Bottles of tomato ketchup

Food was sold in the grocery department. Can you find these groceries?

39

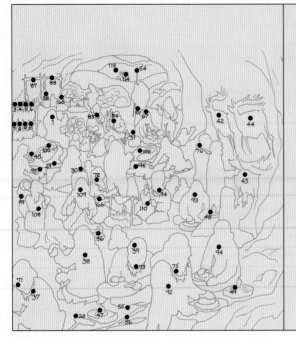

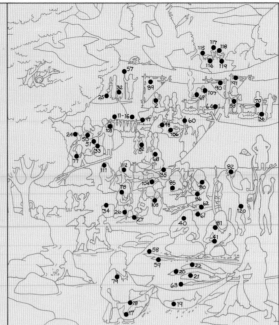

Early people 4–5

Storytellers 1 2
Fish 3 4 5 6 7 8 9
  10 11 12 13 14 15
  16 17 18 19 20
  21 22
Axes 23 24
Digging sticks 25
  26 27
Baskets 28 29 30
  31 32 33 34
  35 36
People chipping
away at flints 37 38
  39 40 41
Deer pictures 42 43
  44
Lamps 45 46 47 48
  49
Leather bags 50 51
  52
Child being dressed
  53
Spears 54 55 56 57
  58 59 60 61 62
  63 64
People cooking 65
  66 67 68 69 70

Necklaces 71 72 73
  74 75 76 77 78
  79 80 81 82
People carving
antlers 83 84 85 86
Wooden racks 87
  88 89 90 91
People making paint
  92 93 94
Skins being scraped
  95 96 97 98
Babies 99 100 101
  102 103 104
  105 106 107
People sewing 108
  109 110 111 112
Wild deer 113
  114 115 116 117
  118 119
Boy who has shot a
bird 120

First farmers 6–7

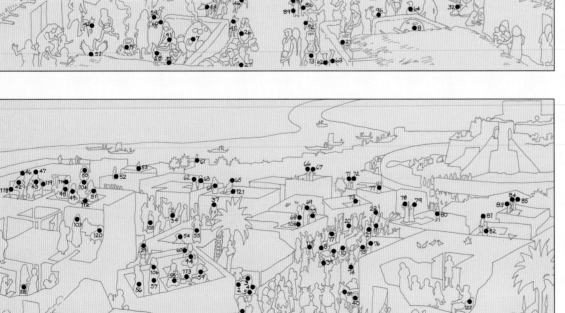

Ovens 1 2 3 4 5
  6 7 8
Ladders 9 10 11
Women with water
pots 12 13 14 15 16
  17 18
Cooking pots 19
  20 21
People fishing 22
  23 24 25
People making pots
  26 27
Men returning from
hunt 28 29
Spindles 30 31 32
Statue 33
Herders 34 35 36
  37
Women grinding 38
  39 40 41
Dogs 42 43 44 45
  46 47 48 49
Children scaring
birds 50 51 52 53
Geese 54 55 56 57
  58 59 60 61 62
  63 64

Cattle 65 66 67 68
  69 70 71 72 73
  74 75 76 77 78
  79 80
Pigs 81 82 83 84
  85 86
Piglets 87 88 89 90
  91 92
Goats 93 94 95 96
Sheep 97 98 99
  100 101 102 103
  104 105 106 107
  108 109 110 111
  112 113 114 115
  116
Looms 117 118 119
Men mending wall
  120 121
Baskets 122 123
  124 125 126 127
  128
Roof on fire 129
Sickles 130 131 132
  133 134

Living in cities 8–9

Scribe 1
Wheels 2 3 4 5 6 7
  8 9 10 11
Soldiers 12 13 14 15
  16 17 18 19 20
  21 22 23 24 25
  26 27
Baskets 28 29 30
  31 32 33 34 35
  36 37 38 39 40
  41
People using straws
  42 43 44 45
People on roofs 46
  47 48 49 50 51
  52 53 54 55 56
  57 58 59 60 61
  62 63 64 65 66
  67 68 69 70 71
  72 73 74 75 76
  77 78 79 80 81
  82 83 84 85
Donkeys with packs
  86 87 88 89
Late boy 90
Stone seal 91
Farmer with sheep
  92

Person who has
broken jar 93
Potter's wheels 94
  95 96 97
King 98
Metalsmiths 99 100
  101
Messenger 102
Women in blue
dresses 103 104
  105 106 107 108
  109 110 111
Pairs of men playing
game 112 113
People playing harps
  114 115 116 117
Chairs 118 119 120
  121 122

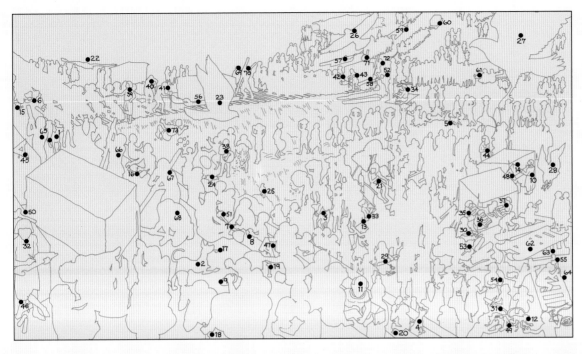

Pyramids 10–11

Dogs 1 2 3 4 5
People polishing 6 7 8 9
Architect 10
Doctor 11
Monkey 12
Pyramid models 13 14
Chisels 15 16 17 18 19 20
King 21
Hawks 22 23 24 25 26 27 28
Saws 29 30 31
Scribes 32 33 34 35 36 37
Man with hole in basket 38
Overseer 39
Oil jars 40 41 42 43
Queen 44
Measuring instruments 45 46 47 48 49
Hammers 50 51 52 53 54 55
Sleds 56 57 58 59 60 61 62 63 64

Men using poles 65 66 67 68 69 70 71 72
Person falling off ramp 73

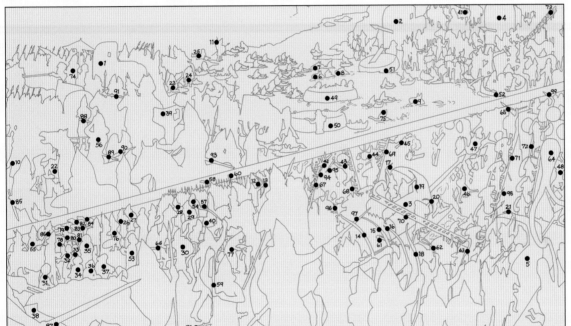

Going into battle 12–13

Siege engines 1 2 3 4 5
Swimming horses 6 7 8 9
Bows 10 11 12 13 14 15 16 17 18 19 20 21
Soldiers putting on boots 22 23 24 25
Soldiers with sacks 26 27 28 29 30
Captives 31 32 33 34 35 36 37
Yellow cloths 38 39 40 41
People falling 42 43 44 45 46 47 48
Boats 49 50 51 52
Scribes 53 54
Soldiers on white horses 55 56
Slings 57 58 59 60 61 62 63 64
Broken spear 65
Ladders 66 67 68 69 70 71 72 73
King 74
Person who has let go of float 75

Person who has dropped shield 76
Mother giving drink to child 77
Sheep 78 79 80 81 82 83 84
Swords 85 86 87 88 89 90 91 92 93 94 95 96 97 98 99

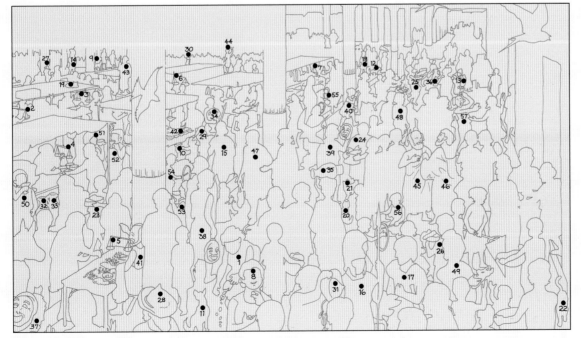

At the market 14–15

Man dropping his money 1
Weighing scales 2 3 4 5 6 7
Person eating olives 8
Dogs 9 10 11 12
Slave carrying too much shopping 13
Soldiers 14 15 16 17 18
Cats 19 20 21 22
People who have been to fish stall 23 24 25 26
Hats 27 28 29 30 31
Two-handled jars 32 33 34 35 36
Actors 37 38 39
Escaping slave 40
Banker 41
Lamp stall 42
Statues 43 44
Philosophers 45 46
People carrying sandals 47 48 49
People drinking wine 50 51 52 53

Children playing with hoops 54 55 56
Man who hates his haircut 57

The bath house 16–17

People having a massage 1 2 3 4	Complaining man 48
People lifting weights 5 6 7 8 9	Strigils 49 50 51 52 53
Person stealing clothes 10	
Caldarium 11	
Statue 12	
Gladiator 13	
Women 14 15 16 17 18	
Man who has forgotten sandals 19	
Thief 20	
Library 21	
Slave who has fainted 22	
Person putting on toga 23	
Frigidarium 24	
Food trays 25 26	
Attendant with towels 27	
Mosaic floor 28	
Soldiers 29 30 31 32 33 34 35 36	
Oil flasks 37 38 39 40 41 42 43 44 45 46 47	

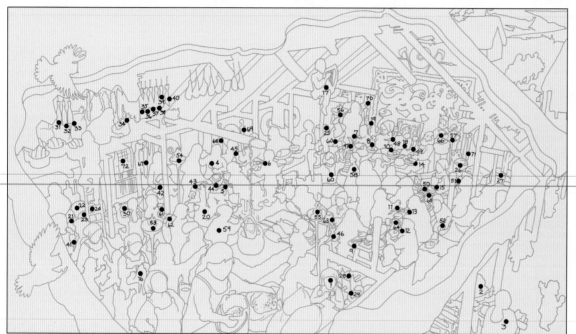

Winter feasts 18–19

Person doing up brooch 1	Person stirring cauldron 59
People fetching wood 2 3	Pair of acrobats 60
Spoons 4 5 6 7 8 9 10 11 12 13 14 15	Jugs 61 62 63 64 65 66
Person with torn tunic 16	Swords 67 68 69 70 71
Poet 17	Loom 72
Chief 18	
Child hiding behind tapestry 19	
Person falling off stool 20	
Barrels 21 22 23 24 25 26 27	
Fighting dogs 28 29	
Open chest 30	
Dried fish 31 32 33 34 35 36 37 38 39 40	
Drinking horns 41 42 43 44 45 46 47 48 49 50 51 52	
Lamps 53 54 55 56 57	
Servant with pile of bowls 58	

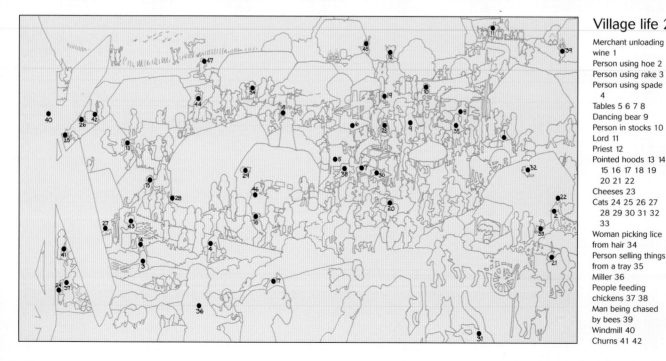

Village life 20–21

Merchant unloading wine 1	People chopping wood 43 44 45
Person using hoe 2	Blacksmith 46
Person using rake 3	Person using stepping stones 47
Person using spade 4	
Tables 5 6 7 8	
Dancing bear 9	
Person in stocks 10	
Lord 11	
Priest 12	
Pointed hoods 13 14 15 16 17 18 19 20 21 22	
Cheeses 23	
Cats 24 25 26 27 28 29 30 31 32 33	
Woman picking lice from hair 34	
Person selling things from a tray 35	
Miller 36	
People feeding chickens 37 38	
Man being chased by bees 39	
Windmill 40	
Churns 41 42	

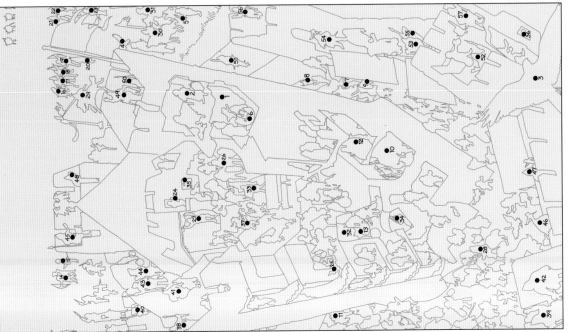

Castle life 22–23

Bed 1
Lord counting money 2
Falcons 3 4 5
Person in a bathtub 6
Horses looking out of stables 7 8 9
Guardroom 10
Candlemaker 11
Chapel 12
Well 13
Archers 14 15 16 17 18 19 20 21 22 23
Person looking out of window 24
Person falling down stairs 25
Group of minstrels 26
Person hanging a tapestry 27
Knights on horseback 28 29 30 31
Storeroom 32
Servant with tray of goblets 33

Prisoner in chains 34
Toilets 35 36
Jester 37
Guards on battlements 38 39 40 41 42 43 44 45 46 47 48 49 50 51 52 53 54 55 56 57

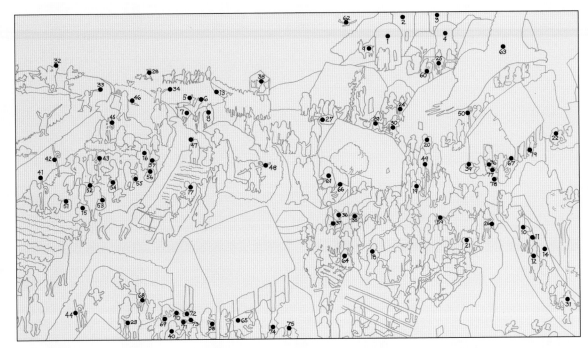

Inca homes 24–25

Storehouses 1 2 3 4
Alpacas 5 6 7 8 9 10 11 12
Bridges 13 14
Babies 15 16 17 18 19 20 21 22
Quipus 23 24 25 26
Llama sitting down 27
Chasquis 28 29 30 31
Pototo 32
Slings 33 34
Panpipes 35
Drum 36
Flute 37
Emperor 38
Cooking pot 39
Woman grinding 40
Digging sticks 41 42 43 44 45 46 47 48 49 50
Sacks of potatoes 51 52 53 54 55 56 57 58 59 60
Person making chicha drink 61
Condors 62 63

Person putting on sandals 64
Looms 65 66 67
Guinea pigs 68 69 70 71 72 73 74 75 76 77 78 79

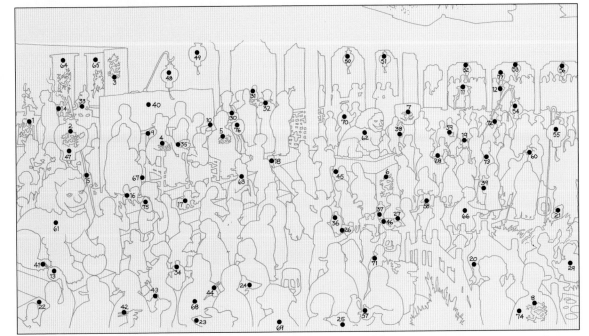

A Chinese party 26–27

Dragon pictures 1 2 3 4 5 6 7 8
Chair covers 9 10 11 12
Half-finished bowl of rice 13
Incense burner 14
Dogs 15 16 17 18 19 20 21
Lacquered trays 22 23 24 25 26 27 28
Gardener and his children 29
Drum 30
Gong 31
Flute 32
Shrine 33
Jars 34 35 36 37 38 39
Screen 40
Pairs of chopsticks 41 42 43 44 45 46
Lanterns 47 48 49 50 51 52 53 54 55 56
Teapots 57 58 59 60

Statues 61 62
Official with boy assistant 63
Paintings 64 65
Servant lighting a firework 66
Red robes 67 68 69 70 71 72 73 74
Fans 75 76 77

Indian wedding 28–29

Elephants 1 2 3 4 5
Holy man 6
Red and gold wall hanging 7
Black and white cushion 8
Blue and green carpet 9
Gardener with spade 10
Throne 11
Man in yellow jama and striped piajamas 12
Dark blue turbans 13 14 15 16 17 18 19 20 21 22
Bride 23
Groom 24
Peacocks 25 26 27 28 29 30
Group of beggars 31
Musician playing sitar 32
Musician playing tambourine 33
Musician playing drum 34

Musician playing brass trumpet 35
Man smoking 36
Dagger with horse's head 37
Palace artist 38
Jade wine cup 39
Silver bowl 40
Emerald necklace 41
Wood and ivory box 42
Person wearing turban jewel 43

Busy ports 30–31

Astrolabe 1
Rope-fitter 2
Sail mender 3
Carpenter 4
Green gable 5
Winches 6 7 8
Sick sailor 9
Open bridge 10
Tulips 11
Scientist using telescope 12
Ivory 13
Silk 14
Porcelain 15
Ladies collecting orphan 16
Servant polishing silver 17
Servant scrubbing floor tiles 18
Servant hanging up laundry 19
Virginal 20
Sailor with wooden leg 21
Swags 22 23 24 25 26 27
Ship owner 28
Guns 29 30 31 32

Artist 33
Sacks of spices 34 35 36

At the ball 32–33

Person whose wig has fallen off 1
Person checking his face in a pocket mirror 2
Embroidered pink shoes 3
Harpsichord 4
King 5
Maid bringing smelling salts to her mistress 6
Arched mirrors 7 8 9 10 11
Dancer who has fallen over 12
Person spilling wine 13
Women peeping over fans 14 15 16 17 18 19 20 21 22 23 24
Person who has misbehaved 25
Chicken 26
Salmon 27
Oranges 28
Couch 29

Chandeliers 30 31 32 33 34
Women with beauty spots 35 36 37 38
Women wearing flowers in their hair 39 40 41 42 43 44 45 46 47 48 49
Man in blue jacket and green breeches 50
Pink dresses 51 52 53 54 55 56 57 58
Servant pouring wine 59
Clocks 60 61

Factory town 34–35

Hansom cabs 1 2
Barges 3 4 5
Person pumping water 6
Person selling coal 7
Person selling fruit and vegetables 8
Person selling milk 9
Workhouse 10
Train 11
Miners 12 13 14 15 16 17
Beggars 18
Rat-catcher 19
Barrel organ player 20
Person selling flowers 21
Person lighting lamps 22
Person selling pies 23
Policemen 24 25 26 27 28 29
Paper-seller 30
Sleeping factory worker 31

Gas lamps 32 33 34 35 36 37 38 39 40 41
Tailor's 42
Barber's 43
Shoemaker's 44
Chimney sweeps 45 46 47
Child selling matches 48

Prairie homes 36–37

Sheriff 1
Person buying lamp 2
Teacher 3
Church 4
Telegraph poles 5 6 7 8 9 10
Family loading their wagon 11
Doctor 12
Place where train stops 13
Cowboys 14 15 16 17 18 19 20 21 22
Buggies 23 24
Newspaper office 25
Men laying new tracks 26 27 28 29 30
Native Americans 31 32 33 34
Guitar 35
Piano 36
Accordion 37

Wagons with covers 38 39 40
Wagons without covers 41 42 43
Barman 44
Guns 45 46 47 48 49 50 51 52
Robbers 53 54
Blacksmith 55

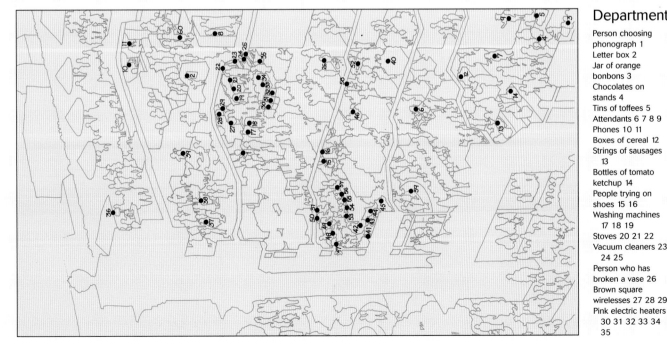

Department stores 38–39

Person choosing phonograph 1
Letter box 2
Jar of orange bonbons 3
Chocolates on stands 4
Tins of toffees 5
Attendants 6 7 8 9
Phones 10 11
Boxes of cereal 12
Strings of sausages 13
Bottles of tomato ketchup 14
People trying on shoes 15 16
Washing machines 17 18 19
Stoves 20 21 22
Vacuum cleaners 23 24 25
Person who has broken a vase 26
Brown square wirelesses 27 28 29
Pink electric heaters 30 31 32 33 34 35

Soda fountain 36
People having their hair cut 37 38 39
Place where people are buying baby clothes 40
Red pedal cars 41 42 43 44 45 46
Grey rocking horses 47 48 49 50 51 52
Teddy bears 53 54 55 56 57 58
Fashion show 59
Person buying orange book 60

What are they doing?

You can find each of these people somewhere in the little pictures earlier in this book. To do this puzzle, you'll need to look back and find where they come from.

1. Which of these people is painting a picture?

A B C D E F

2. Which of these children is late for school?

A B C D E F

3. Which of these people is going into battle?

A B C D E F G

4. Which of these women is a queen?

A B C D E F G

5. Which of these people is telling a story?

A B C D E F

6. Which of these pairs of people is in the middle of an argument?

A B C D E

The answers are on page 171.

Test your memory

How much can you remember about this part of the book?
Try doing this quiz to find out. Answers are on page 171.

First farmers

1. How did the first farmers cut down their crops?
   A They used tools called sickles
   B They used large knives
   C They used tools called scythes
   D They used combine harvesters

2. How did the first farmers grind grain into flour?
   A They used a windmill
   B They jumped up and down on it
   C They used a watermill
   D They used two stones

Living in cities

3. What was a ziggurat?
   A A type of donkey
   B A board game
   C A big stepped platform
   D A fastening for clothes

4. What did a scribe do?
   A Sing songs at funerals
   B Teach children
   C Make baskets
   D Read and write for other people

Pyramids

5. How long did it take to build a pyramid?
   A About a year
   B About 5 years
   C About 20 years
   D About 3 months

6. Who planned the building of a pyramid?
   A An overseer
   B An architect
   C A stonemason
   D A carpenter

Going into battle

7. Soldiers on horseback were called?
   A The cavalry
   B The army
   C The horseboys
   D The trotters

8. What did soldiers use as floats to cross rivers?
   A Logs
   B Their wives
   C Inflated animal skins
   D Rubber rings

At the market

9. What was an ancient Greek marketplace called?
   A An agony
   B An agora
   C An angora
   D An ogre

The bath house

10. What did the Romans do with a strigil?
    A They wore it
    B They sat on it
    C They ate it
    D They used it to scrape oil and dirt off their bodies

11. What was the hot room in a Roman baths called?
    A A sauna
    B A frigidarium
    C A caldarium
    D A steamroomium

Winter feasts

12. What was a Viking poet called?
    A A skald
    B A scold
    C A bard
    D A bald

13. What did Viking women use to fasten their tunics?
    A Pins
    B Brooches
    C Buttons
    D Crab claws

20. What did people do with a jama?
    A Read it
    B Kneel on it
    C Ride on it
    D Wear it

Village life
14. What did a blacksmith do?
    A Make and mend locks
    B Grind grain into flour
    C Make and sell tents
    D Make and mend metal tools

Busy ports
21. What was used to measure the height of stars?
    A An astrolabe
    B A gable
    C An astronome
    D A telescope

Castle life
15. What did a jester try to do?
    A Make tapestries
    B Make pastries
    C Make people laugh
    D Make beds

At the ball
22. What were mens' wigs made of?
    A Goat hair
    B Human hair
    C Horse hair
    D Any of the above

Inca homes
16. What was a chasquis?
    A An Incan kiss chase
    B A rope bridge
    C A cooking pot
    D A messenger

Factory town
23. Where were homeless children sent?
    A To a hotel
    B To Australia
    C To a workhouse
    D To bed

17. What was a quipu?
    A An animal
    B A joke
    C A musical instrument
    D A knotted string

Prairie homes
24. What shape was a sheriff's badge?
    A Star-shaped
    B Moon-shaped
    C Pear-shaped
    D Square-shaped

A Chinese party
18. What was porcelain?
    A A drink made from rice
    B Cloth made from pig bristles
    C A type of pottery
    D A type of tea

25. What did men do in a saloon?
    A Ride horses
    B Drink and play cards
    C Worship
    D Travel

Indian wedding
19. What would you do with a sitar?
    A Eat it
    B Sit on it
    C Play it
    D Put it on your head

Department stores
26. What was a wireless?
    A An early computer
    B A telephone
    C A new kind of underwear
    D A radio

Answers on page 171

THE GREAT WORLD SEARCH

Illustrated by David Hancock

Contents

About the World Search

Great Aunt Marigold has given you a wonderful present: a ticket to go on a trip around the world. You will visit lots of exciting places and there are all kinds of things to find and puzzles to solve along the way.

This is Great Aunt Marigold. She'll be coming with you on the trip.

This map of the world shows the places you will stop at on your tour.

Great Aunt Marigold says that in each place, you have to pick up a present for a friend or relation. But she hasn't told you which present is in which place – that's one of the puzzles for you to solve. Here's what you have to find:

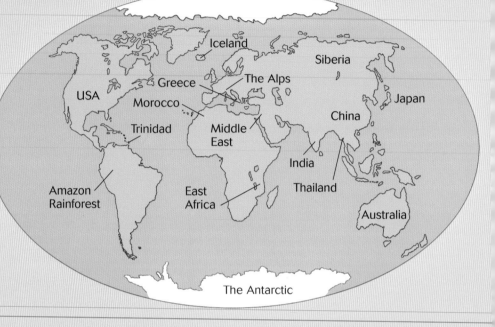

Iceland
Siberia
Greece
The Alps
USA
Morocco
Japan
China
Trinidad
Middle East
India
Thailand
Amazon Rainforest
East Africa
Australia
The Antarctic

Bunch of bananas for Baby Nina

Big box of chocolates for Great Uncle Frank

Wooden fan for Jo

Cheese for Lennox the mouse

Striped gloves for Sacha

Spotted ball for Sniff the dog

Mirror for Mrs. Choy

Painted parasol for Rosie

Clay statue for Doctor Parekh

Yellow cushion for Muffin the cat

T-shirt for Max

Green flippers for Aunt Mimi

Bath salts for Jack

Blue binoculars for Uncle Mike

Radio for the twins

White furry hat for Mr. Choy

Garland of flowers for Great Aunt Eva

What to spot

Every double page in this part of the book shows a different place on your tour. In each place, there are lots of things to look for. Some things are easy to spot, but some are tricky. This is how the puzzles work.

This strip tells you where you are, what time it is, and what the weather's like.

This tells you what Great Aunt Marigold is doing. You'll find her in every place.

Around the edge of the big picture, there are lots of little pictures.

The writing next to each little picture tells you how many of that thing you can find in the big picture.

You can only see part of this train, but it still counts.

This box is a reminder of the presents you have to find. There's one present in each place.

This tells you to find something you'll need in the next place.

Finding the way

When you've done all the puzzles on a double page, you have to find out where to go next – it won't be the place on the next page. You also need to find how to travel there. Here's what you do:

   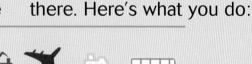   

In the bottom right-hand corner of each double page, four tiny pictures tell you how to travel to the next place.

To find out where to go next, look for exactly the same four pictures in the top left-hand corner of another double page.

You'll travel by train, plane, boat or bus, but you won't use them all on each journey, and you may use any of them more than once.

PUZZLE CHECKLIST

In each place, you must find:
~ Great Aunt Marigold
~ One present for a friend or relation
~ Lots of things hidden in the big picture
~ One thing you'll need in the next place
~ Which place to go to next

If you get stuck finding your way, there's a map showing the correct route on page 88. If you get stuck doing any of the other puzzles, you'll find all the answers on pages 90–95. Now turn the page and begin your journey...

Great Aunt Marigold has lots of bags. Find her.

3:30PM...GREAT WORLD TOUR NOW BOARDING

At the airport

Information about flights is displayed on screens. Can you spot 11?

You can shop for all kinds of things. Find someone buying sunglasses.

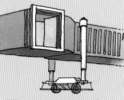

To get onto the plane, you go along a covered walkway. Can you see where it is?

Restaurants serve food and drink. Can you spot someone eating this meal?

Old or disabled people can be driven around in buggies. Spot two.

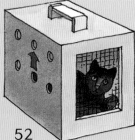

Some kinds of pets can be taken on planes, but only in special containers. Find this cat.

You're setting off on your exciting trip from a big, busy airport. Outside, the plane is filling up with people. Before getting on board, you must check in your bags and go through security. Then you'll be off!

Bag being searched

Knife showing up on X-ray machine

Security officers check that no one has any weapons. Find these things.

Person going through metal detector

52

PRESENT CHECKLIST

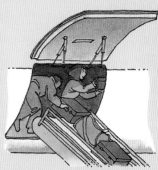

Bags that have been checked in are loaded into the cargo hold of the plane. Find it.

You need a ticket to go on a plane journey. Spot someone who has torn his ticket.

You can wheel your bags around on a trolley. Can you spot seven?

At the bureau de change, you can buy money to use in other countries. Can you find it?

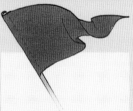

In the first place on your tour, there will be a festival. Find a red flag to wave.

Spot eight telephones.

Flight attendants look after the passengers on planes. Find ten.

Officers in the control tower give instructions to the pilots of the planes. Can you see it?

Great Aunt Marigold is dropping her shopping. Find her.

Floating market

A straw hat will protect you from the sun. Spot two boats selling hats.

Most fruit and vegetables are sold by weight. Spot nine sets of weighing scales.

Can you find 11 purple-throated sunbirds?

You can buy curry with noodles or rice. Find two boats where food is being cooked and sold.

You've taken a trip along a canal to visit this unusual market. Most things here are being sold from boats. If you want to buy something, just call out to the person in the boat. She'll paddle over and you can do your shopping.

Can you spot someone who is selling grilled corn on the cob?

Watermelons

Pineapples

Lots of fresh fruit and vegetables are for sale. Find two boats full of each of these.

Coconuts

Limes

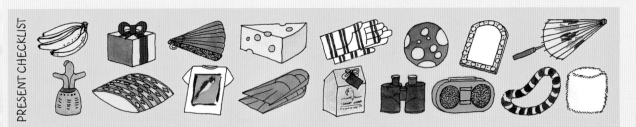

Dolls dressed as traditional Thai dancers are for sale. Can you see where?

Flowers

Pots and pans

Fish

Find three boats selling each of these things in the market.

Buddhist temple

Buddhism is the main religion here, so there are lots of Buddhist temples. Spot one.

In the next place, you'll be going out for the evening. Find this silk jacket to wear.

You can buy all kinds of beautiful handmade crafts. Can you spot these things?

Embroidered cushions

Carved wooden tables

Silver necklaces

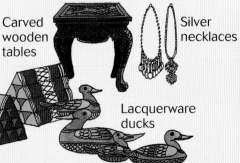

Lacquerware ducks

Buddhist monks come out of their temples to ask for food. Spot six.

AUSTRALIA...1:30PM...24°C/75°F...WINDY

Great Aunt Marigold is being very active. Can you see her?

On the beach

Windsurfers sail along, standing on a sailboard. Find ten.

Sunblock

Sunblock protects your skin from the sun. Spot four people putting it on.

Dolphins are very friendly and often swim near people. Spot ten.

Kayak

Speedboat

Sailboat

There are all kinds of boats here. Find seven of each of these.

Spot 14 seagulls.

It's a hot, sunny summer's day and you've arrived at a very crowded beach. You could go for a swim, or join all the people doing exciting sports in the water. If you're feeling lazy, you could just lie on the sand and relax.

Water-skiers are pulled along the surface of the water by a speedboat. Spot eight.

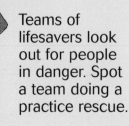

Teams of lifesavers look out for people in danger. Spot a team doing a practice rescue.

You can go diving around coral reefs to look at the amazing underwater wildlife. Spot five divers.

PRESENT CHECKLIST

Flags mark out which areas are safe from sharks or dangerous tides. Spot two.

Koala

Kangaroo

Kangaroos and koalas live in the wild in Australia. Can you find a toy one of each?

Surfers skim over the waves on a surfboard. Find 30.

People drive jet skis across the water. Spot nine.

In the next place, there are some unusual birds. Find a camera to take pictures of them.

You can breathe through a snorkel when you swim with your face in the water. Spot ten snorkels. Snorkel

Parasailers have parachutes. A boat pulls them along on the water and they rise into the air. Spot two.

Great Aunt Marigold is being helpful. Can you see where she is?

Desert homes

The Bedouin take good care of their camels and often give them names. Can you spot 40?

Bedouin foods include meat, rice, cheese and bread. Find someone baking bread.

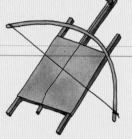

These musical instruments, called rababs, are often played to entertain guests. Find four.

Goats are kept for meat, and their thick hair is woven to make tents. Spot 30.

You've journeyed across the dry, dusty desert to visit the Bedouin people. They usually live in small groups, but today they've come together to prepare for a big festival. The tents are buzzing with all kinds of activity.

Sahah

In each tent, the men's area and the women's area are separated by a curtain, called a sahah. Find four.

Sacks of dried food

Strings of onions

The Bedouin sell animals and buy some things at markets in towns. Find three of each of these things.

Metal cooking pots

Women weave rugs, saddlebags, cushions and cloth from goat or camel hair. Find this rug.

Today, most Bedouin travel in trucks instead of on camels. Can you find nine?

Fast dogs, called salukis, hunt hares for their owners. Spot ten.

People drink frothy camel milk and also use it for cooking. Spot three bowls of it.

In the next place, you can visit temples. Spot a book telling you where they are.

The Bedouin make coffee for anyone who visits their tent. Find these things.

Coffee pot

Ladle for roasting coffee

Coffee cups

Pestle and mortar for grinding coffee

Can you find three camel saddles?

Great Aunt Marigold has stopped for a bite to eat. Can you find her?

City lights

You've arrived in the middle of this noisy, bustling city in Japan. It's just beginning to get dark so the lights are on.

There are crowds of people everywhere you look. Some are enjoying an evening out and others are rushing home.

Can you spot 20 schoolchildren with their backpacks?

Sushi is a special dish of cold rice and raw fish. Can you see where it is for sale?

Spot six people wearing masks to avoid giving their colds to others.

You can buy food on the street. Find a stall selling grilled chicken.

People bow to say "hello" and "goodbye". Spot 14 people bowing.

Vending machines sell all kinds of things, such as magazines, tickets, noodles and drinks. Find seven.

In a karaoke bar, you can sing into a microphone while a tape plays background music. Spot one.

Microphone

Sumo wrestlers need to be big and strong to win matches. Find four.

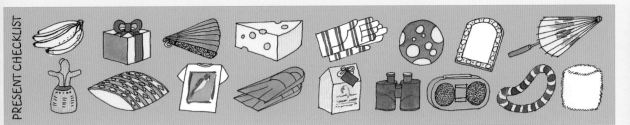

PRESENT CHECKLIST

Capsule hotels have tiny cubicles instead of rooms. Spot someone asleep in a cubicle.

You can buy all sorts of electronic equipment here. Find a place selling computers.

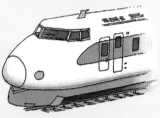

Very fast trains, called bullet trains, have pointed fronts. Spot three.

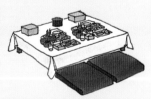

In a traditional restaurant, you need to sit at low tables, on mats on the floor. Spot one.

You're going swimming in the next place on your tour. Find a towel.

Traditional dresses called kimonos are mainly worn on special occasions. Spot 16.

People worship at temples and shrines. Can you spot one of each?

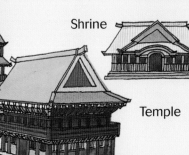

Shrine

Temple

At the pool

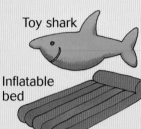

All kinds of birds make their nests on nearby coasts. Spot 20 eider ducks.

Toy shark

Inflatable bed

Many people just come to relax and have fun in the water. Find seven of each of these.

Buoys show you where the water's too hot to swim in, and where it's very shallow. Spot 20.

A power station next to the pool uses steam from the hot water. Can you find five pipes blowing out steam?

Great Aunt Marigold is trying to read. Can you see where she is?

You can have fun splashing around in this pool called the Blue Lagoon. The hot, salty water comes up from under the ground. Nearby, there are bubbling mud pools and springs that spout steam and boiling water into the air.

Horse riding

There are lots of activities to do in the area. Spot seven people doing each of these things.

Hiking

At the Blue Lagoon Clinic, doctors treat people who have skin problems. Can you see a doctor?

Skincare products are for sale here. Find someone who has bought lots of tubes of face cream.

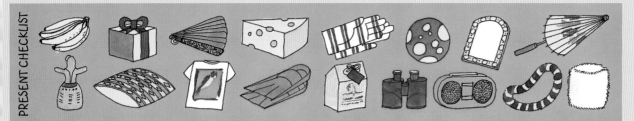

Trucks are good for driving on Iceland's bumpy roads. Spot eight.

These food trays contain Icelandic fish, such as shark, shrimp or salmon. Spot 21.

There are changing rooms where you can leave your clothes. Find the women's one.

You can stay at the Blue Lagoon Hotel. Spot a man who's just arrived with lots of bags.

Next, you're going on a boat. Find some sea-sickness pills in case you feel ill.

Waiters and waitresses serve people food and drink in the water. Spot four of each.

Both the water and the mud at the bottom of the pool are supposed to be good for your skin. Spot 15 people with mud on their faces.

Great Aunt Marigold is wrapped up warmly. Can you see her?

Frozen land

Albatrosses glide over the water looking for food. Find three.

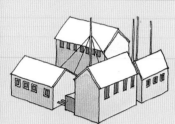

No one lives here all the time, but scientists stay at the research station. Find it.

Killer whales sometimes hunt seals by tipping them off pieces of ice. Spot four.

Castle

Pyramid

Greek temple

Icebergs are huge lumps of ice that float in the sea. Can you find these shapes?

"Porpoising" out of the water

"Tobogganing" across the ice

You've come to the cold, windy Antarctic, where the land and sea are nearly always frozen. You can watch whales and take photos of penguins, but you mustn't disturb the animals or spoil their icy home.

Penguins can't fly, but they have other ways of moving fast. Find 12 penguins doing each of these things.

Scientists dive into the icy water to watch animals and take pictures. Find seven divers.

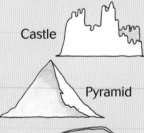

Spot 12 crabeater seals.

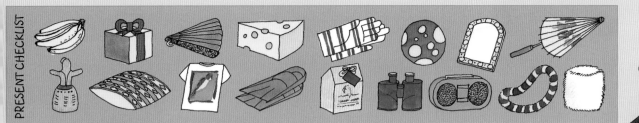

Scientists go in small planes to do research in very remote areas. Find three.

Find one humpback whale.

Small boats called dinghies are good for finding a way through the icy sea. Spot eight.

Leopard seals are fierce. They often hunt penguins. Can you spot two?

Next, you'll be going to a shady place. Find a flashlight to help you see.

Research ships carry scientists and their supplies. Cruise ships carry tourists. Spot one of each.

Research ship

Cruise ship

Scientists attach satellite tags to some large animals, to record information about how they live. Spot two.

Carnival!

You've arrived just in time for the Carnival. Hundreds of people are parading along the street in big groups. You can have fun just watching them go by, but the music is so lively, you're bound to start dancing.

PRESENT CHECKLIST

Great Aunt Marigold is dancing in the crowd. Can you see her?

Underwater

The circus

Incas

Flying animals

Spanish dancing

Each group has a theme, and the members' costumes show what it is. Find the groups with these themes.

Many costumes cost a lot and take months to make. Spot this amazing one.

The police make sure there is no trouble. Spot ten police officers.

Some musicians travel on trucks called floats. Spot three.

These metal drums are called pans. Spot 18.

Moco Jumbie

Burroquite

Jab Molassi

Some traditional characters are here every year. Find these.

Next, you'll be doing lots of shopping. Find a calculator to add up what you spend.

Tasty tropical fruits, such as mangoes and pineapples, grow in Trinidad. Find a fruit stall.

Carnival songs, called calypsos, have a strong beat and are good to dance to. Spot two people singing into microphones.

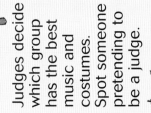

The coconut seller slices the top off coconuts, so you can drink the juice and scoop out the soft, white flesh. Find her.

Cups of fruit sorbet

Corn on the cob

Bread called roti

Can you see where people are selling these snacks on the street?

Judges decide which group has the best music and costumes. Spot someone pretending to be a judge.

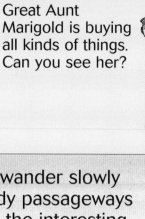

Great Aunt Marigold is buying all kinds of things. Can you see her?

Shady souk

Herbs and spices, such as mint and saffron, look and smell wonderful. Find where they are being sold.

Lute

Drum

You can often hear music in the souk. Find these instruments.

Wool for making carpets is dyed and hung up to dry. Spot three people carrying bundles of wool.

Dates grow in the desert, on date palm trees. Can you see some dates for sale?

You've arrived in the middle of a busy Moroccan market, called a souk. There are lots of unusual things for sale. You can wander slowly down the shady passageways and take in all the interesting sights, smells and noises.

Painted pottery

Copper trays

Woven baskets

Embroidered caps

Leather slippers called babouches

You can buy lovely handmade crafts and may even see some being made. Find where these things are being sold.

Horse riding has been popular here for hundreds of years. Spot two saddles for sale.

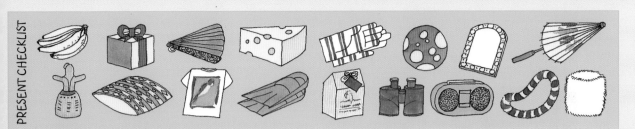

Water carriers go around selling cups of water to thirsty shoppers. Spot four.

Live animals are on sale. Find nine chickens.

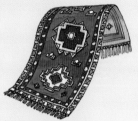

People argue over the price of things. Spot two people bargaining for this carpet.

Can you spot where olives are being sold from huge baskets?

In the next place, you might sit out in the hot sun. Find a shady hat to wear.

While you are deciding what to buy, the stall holder may offer you a glass of hot mint tea. Spot seven glasses.

Women buy powder for making up their eyes, lips and cheeks, and cedarwood containers to keep it in. Spot 12 containers.

Cedarwood container

Bottles of powder

At the mall

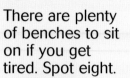

Great Aunt Marigold has bought lots of things. Can you find her?

There are plenty of benches to sit on if you get tired. Spot eight.

At the information desk, people will help you find what you need. Can you see it?

The mall is so big, it's easy to get lost. Find a child who has lost his mother.

You can have your hair washed and cut at the hair salon. Can you spot it?

At this big, busy mall, you can do all your shopping without ever having to go outside. If you don't want to shop, you can eat or drink instead. Some people come to the mall to meet their friends and have a chat.

Kites

Books

Cowboy hats

Flowers

Jeans

Shoes

Sports equipment

Can you find where these things are for sale?

Cakes

Can you spot a group of cheerleaders putting on a show?

70

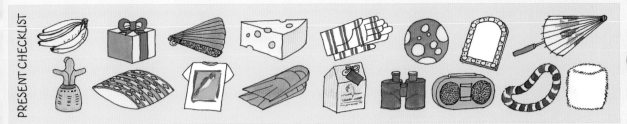

Paintings, called murals, make the walls look bright and interesting. Can you see one?

You can travel from one level to another in the glass elevator. Can you find it?

Spot five telephones.

Security guards check that there is no trouble in the mall. Spot ten.

In the next place, you might stay in a hotel. Find a new suitcase to put your things in.

You can buy lots of different foods here. Can you see where people are eating these things?

Spaghetti
Ice cream
Pizza

Statues, plants and fountains make you feel as if you're outside. Spot 24 flamingo statues.

Going skiing

Snowmobiles are like little cars on skis. Spot five.

Goggles protect your eyes from the sun. Can you see someone who has broken his goggles?

Chairlift

Gondola

Chairlifts and gondolas take you to the top of steep slopes. Find four of each of these.

You can ride through the snow in a horse-drawn sleigh. Spot three.

Great Aunt Marigold isn't a very good skier. Can you see where she is?

This crowded ski resort is one of the liveliest places on your tour. You can have all kinds of fun skiing down the snowy slopes. There are lots of other sporty things to do too. But be careful that you don't bump into anyone.

There are kindergarten groups for children who are too young to ski. Spot two groups building snowmen.

Snowboarders use one wide board instead of two skis. Spot ten.

Snowboard

If you don't have your own skis, you can rent them. Find a ski-rental shop.

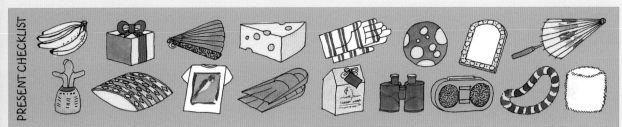

Paraskiers ski off mountains and float to the ground using a parachute. Find three.

Teachers called ski instructors give people skiing lessons. Spot two.

You can go sliding down the slopes on a toboggan. Find nine.

On gentle slopes, a drag lift pulls you up to the top. Spot three people on a drag lift.

In the next place, you'll be doing lots of shopping. Find this useful shopping bag.

Some people go climbing up the mountains. Spot three climbers with ice picks.

Ice pick

On frozen lakes, you can skate and play sports. Spot 30 people on skates.

There are hang-gliders in the sky. Spot three.

On safari

Great Aunt Marigold is about to take a photo. Can you see her?

When they spot a dead animal, vultures fly down to feed on it. Can you find 14?

Baboons live in groups called troops. They all look after the babies. Find 23.

Baobab trees store lots of water in their trunks. Spot two.

Cheetahs creep up on other animals before chasing them. Find five.

Agama lizards scuttle around in the grass or on rocks. Spot three.

Here, you're out in the open air, on the hot, dry, African plains. You've joined lots of other people on an exciting animal-watching trip called a safari. It's hard to believe there are so many amazing animals living in one place.

Hot-air balloon

Bus

On a safari, you can travel around in different ways. Spot three of each of these.

Truck

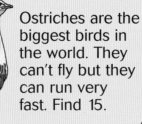

Ostriches are the biggest birds in the world. They can't fly but they can run very fast. Find 15.

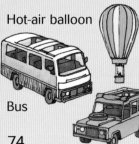

Insects called termites build nests inside huge mounds of soil. Find four termite mounds.

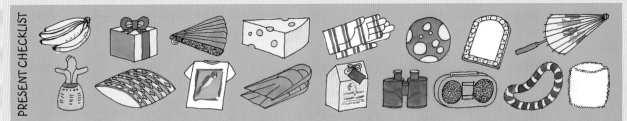

Weaverbirds make complicated nests out of lots of pieces of grass. Spot ten.

Lions like to lie in the shade. Can you find nine?

Zebra

Thomson's gazelle

Wildebeest

These animals eat grass nearly all day long. Spot 15 of each of them.

Scientists come here to find out about wildlife. Can you spot four?

You're going to an even drier place next. Find a bottle of water to take with you.

Wild dogs hunt together in groups called packs. Spot nine.

Elephants are so big, they need to eat a lot. Find 17.

Giraffes have to bend a long way down to reach water. Spot 13.

Great Aunt Marigold is busy making friends. Can you see her?

Town life

In this pretty town, there's a canal to walk along and some lovely gardens. As you wander around, you'll see people getting ready for the New Year Festival. They are shopping for presents and making decorations.

At the New Year, some people dress up and parade along the street. Find a dragon costume.

Pigs

Ducks

Can you see these animals being taken to market?

In China, there are steam trains, and newer diesel or electric trains too. Spot a steam train.

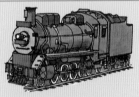

Many Chinese people are farmers. Spot ten farmers growing rice in paddy fields.

Tea grows in lots of parts of China and is a popular drink. Spot some teapots for sale.

Most people travel around the town on bicycles. Find 20.

Silk thread comes from caterpillars called silkworms. People weave it into soft cloth. Find some rolls of silk cloth.

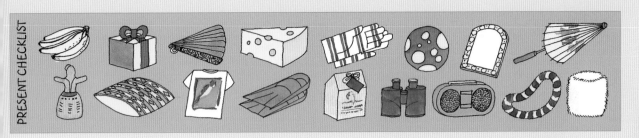

Giant pandas are very rare animals. Wild ones live only in China. Find a toy panda.

Some people keep birds. Find seven birdcages.

Find a group of people doing exercises called t'ai chi.

Many things are made out of bamboo. Can you find three of these bamboo baby buggies?

There will be lots of snow in the next place. Find a spade to clear a path.

A pagoda is a kind of tall tower. It's usually part of a temple. Can you see one?

Spot nine people carrying things in baskets hanging from a pole across their shoulders.

Find three kites.

Great Aunt Marigold is sitting in the shade. Find her.

Forest people

The Ashaninca travel up and down the river in canoes. They fish from them too. Find nine.

People paint their faces with red dye from the seeds of anatto plants. Spot a girl with an armful of anatto seeds.

Mothers often carry their babies in slings. Find nine babies in slings.

Many beautiful birds live in the forest. Some are kept as pets. Spot a girl with a pet parrot.

You've paddled up the River Amazon, right into the heart of the hot, sticky rainforest. The people living here are called the Ashaninca. They gather plants from the forest, hunt animals for food, and grow their own crops.

The main food is a plant called cassava, which is made into flour. Spot someone mashing up cassava with a pole.

Men go hunting with bows and arrows. Find 11 bows.

The big thatched roofs are made from palm leaves. Can you see someone mending a roof?

78

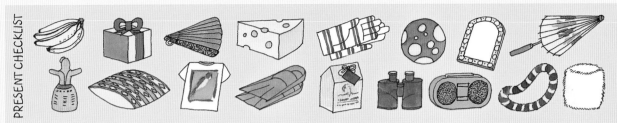

Families of red howler monkeys live in the forest. Spot 18 monkeys.

People sleep in hammocks. Can you find seven?

Wood is used to make houses, ladders, canoes, weapons and tools. Find someone chopping wood.

Children use catapults to shoot at birds. Find two.

Next, you're going to a big party. Find a feather garland to wear.

Houses are built on stilts above the ground, so people use ladders to climb up to them. Spot two ladders.

The Ashaninca grow cotton to make clothes, hammocks and slings. Find two people doing each of these things.

Spinning cotton into thread

Weaving thread into cloth

Great Aunt Marigold is busy exploring the island. Can you see where she is?

Island life

Donkeys are used for carrying things. Find eight.

Modern vases are often made to look like ancient Greek ones. Spot six big vases like this.

This musical instrument is a bouzouki. Can you find eight?

Yogurt and banana

Stuffed vine leaves

Greek salad

Restaurants serve delicious food. Spot someone eating this meal.

Churches often have dome-shaped roofs. Find three.

This pretty island looks like an exciting place to stop for a while. You can explore the winding alleyways or climb up to the old castle on the hill. There are lots of people here. Some live on the island, and some are just visiting.

Women make lace and embroider cloths. They decorate their homes with these. Spot ten women sewing.

Leather bags

Necklaces

Can you see where these are being sold?

Postcards

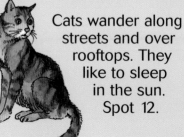

Cats wander along streets and over rooftops. They like to sleep in the sun. Spot 12.

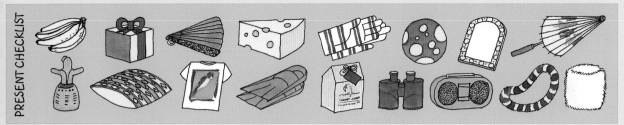

You can learn about Greek history by visiting ruined buildings. Find some ruins.

The only way to leave the island is by boat. Can you spot five little boats with oars?

Mediterranean monk seals are so rare, they are hardly ever seen. Can you find two?

When they are closed, shutters keep houses cool. Spot 11 windows with red shutters.

In the next place, you'll see lots of animals. Find a pad and crayons to draw them.

Many islanders make money from fishing. Find four of each of these things.

Fishing boats

Baskets of fish

Can you spot these people working?

Shoemaker

Baker

Tinsmith

Great Aunt Marigold is stuck in traffic. Can you see her?

On the street

You've arrived in the middle of the hustle and bustle of an Indian town. The streets are full of traffic and swarming with crowds. Plenty of rich people live here, but other people are so poor, they have to beg for money.

Monkeys, called langurs, scamper around the town, looking for food. Can you find 20?

Trains are often so crowded that people have to sit on top. Spot one.

Cycle rickshaw

Scooter rickshaw

Rickshaws are used as taxis. Spot eight of each of these types.

To say "hello", you put your hands together and bow your head. Spot 12 pairs of people saying hello.

The old fort was built hundreds of years ago, to protect the town from enemies. Can you see it?

Tea is boiled in a pan with milk and sugar. Spices are often added. Spot the tea seller.

Can you spot 16 crows?

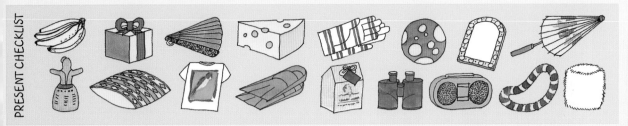

The cinema is very popular. Find this poster telling people what's on.

Can you see where these tasty sweetmeats are being sold?

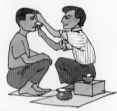

The street barber doesn't charge much to shave people. Find him.

A puri is a type of bread which is fried until it puffs up into a ball. Spot a man frying puris.

In the next place, the ground might be wet. Find a pair of deck shoes so you don't slip.

To worship, Hindus go to temples and Muslims go to mosques. Find one of each.

Temple

Mosque

Most Indians are Hindus. They believe that cows are holy, so let them wander wherever they want. Spot seven cows.

Great Aunt Marigold is admiring the reindeer. Can you see her?

Reindeer races

Dogs called laikas are used to pull sleds. Their thick coats keep them warm. Spot 32.

Balalaika

Accordion

Musicians entertain people at the races. Spot six of each of these musical instruments.

People fill oil drums with ice from the river. They melt it for water. Spot 20.

Siberia is very hard to get to. People often arrive here by helicopter. Can you spot two?

You've journeyed all the way north to Siberia. Everyone is celebrating the end of the long, cold winter with reindeer races on the frozen river. Many people here keep herds of reindeer. They make warm clothes from their skins.

Some herders follow their reindeer around as they look for food. They live in tents called chums. Find three.

Frozen rivers make good ice rinks. Can you spot 15 people skating?

There are huge forests in Siberia, so people make things out of wood. Spot three people chopping wood.

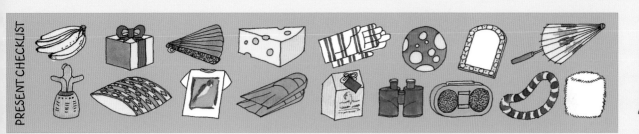

A samovar is a big metal pot for making tea. Can you see one?

Reindeer herders carve beautiful things from bone. Can you see someone carving?

Wild bears, wolves, elk and sable live in nearby forests. Find a toy bear.

Sliding along on skis is often easier than walking on snow. Spot ten people on skis.

The next place is cold and snowy too. Find some warm, furry earmuffs.

Trucks are good for driving on icy ground. Snowmobiles are used for shorter journeys. Find six of each.

Snowmobile

Truck

For the races, reindeer wear bright cloths and harnesses. Find someone dressing up his reindeer.

Can you find Mr. Choy trying on his white furry hat?

Cruising along

Muffin seems to like her yellow cushion. See if you can spot her.

Baby Nina is munching her bananas. Can you find her?

Great Aunt Eva loves her garland of flowers. Can you see where she is?

A painted parasol was just what Rosie wanted. Can you see her?

The last part of your journey is a trip on this luxury cruise ship. There are lots of things to do here. As a surprise, Great Aunt Marigold has invited all your friends and relations. Can you spot them with their presents?

Can you spot Jack with his bath salts?

Jo is keeping cool with her fan. Find her.

Uncle Mike is looking out to sea through his blue binoculars. Can you find him?

Great Uncle Frank is already eating his chocolates. Can you see where he is?

Aunt Mimi is having fun with her flippers. Look hard and see if you can spot her.

Max is wearing his new T-shirt to play with some friends. Find him.

Spot Doctor Parekh chatting to someone about her clay statue.

Find the twins listening to their radio together.

Spot Sacha showing off his striped gloves.

Lennox is nibbling his cheese. Can you spot him?

Mrs. Choy is very pleased with her mirror. Can you see where she is?

Sniff is playing with his spotted ball. Find him.

Your tour is over! To say "thank you" to Great Aunt Marigold, you've bought her a new dress. Can you see her wearing it?

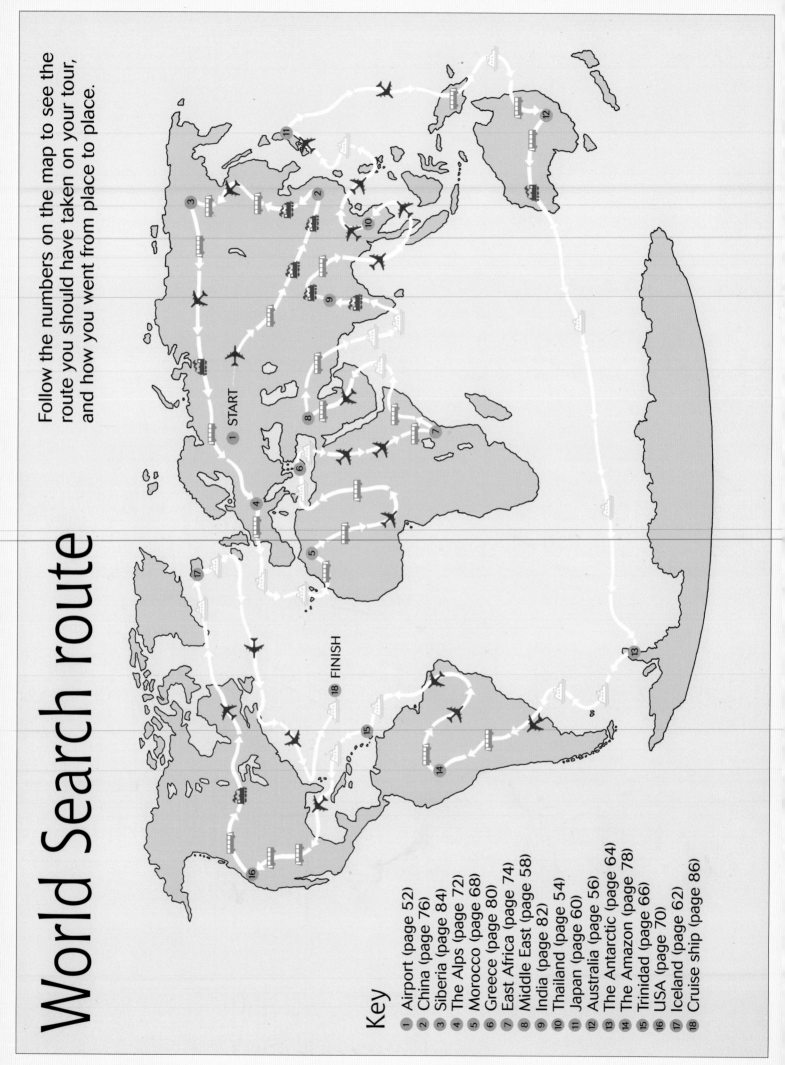

World Search route

Follow the numbers on the map to see the route you should have taken on your tour, and how you went from place to place.

START

FINISH

Key

1. Airport (page 52)
2. China (page 76)
3. Siberia (page 84)
4. The Alps (page 72)
5. Morocco (page 68)
6. Greece (page 80)
7. East Africa (page 74)
8. Middle East (page 58)
9. India (page 82)
10. Thailand (page 54)
11. Japan (page 60)
12. Australia (page 56)
13. The Antarctic (page 64)
14. The Amazon (page 78)
15. Trinidad (page 66)
16. USA (page 70)
17. Iceland (page 62)
18. Cruise ship (page 86)

Extra puzzle

To do this puzzle, you'll need to look back through the book. Don't forget to look at the information strips on each double page. If you get stuck, you'll find the answers on page 171.

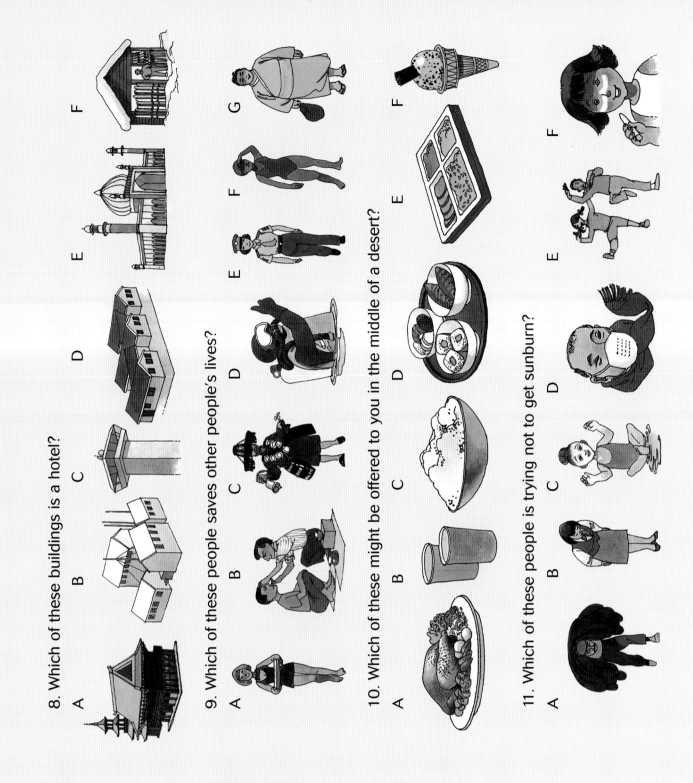

1. Which was the coldest place you visited?

2. Which was the hottest place you visited?

3. What was the earliest time you had to get up?

4. Which place were you in at 3:30pm?

5. How many snowy places did you visit?

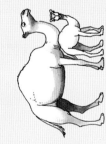

6. How many sunny places did you visit?

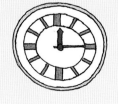

7. How many of each of these did you go on?

8. Which of these buildings is a hotel?

A   B   C   D   E   F

9. Which of these people saves other people's lives?

A   B   C   D   E   F   G

10. Which of these might be offered to you in the middle of a desert?

A   B   C   D   E   F

11. Which of these people is trying not to get sunburn?

A   B   C   D   E   F

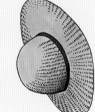

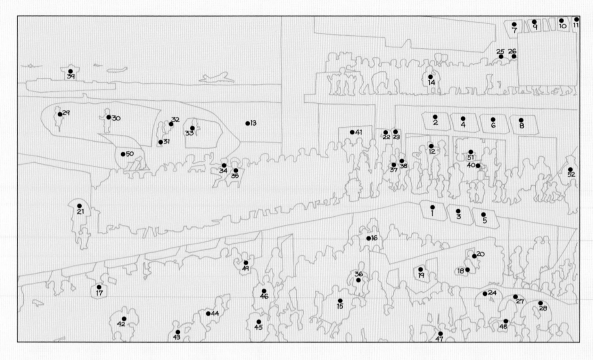

At the airport 52–53

Screens 1 2 3 4 5 6
7 8 9 10 11
Person buying
sunglasses 12
Covered walkway 13
Person eating meal
14
Buggies 15 16
Cat 17
Bag being searched
18
Knife on X-ray
machine 19
Person going
through metal
detector 20
Phones 21 22 23
24 25 26 27 28
Flight attendants 29
30 31 32 33 34
35 36 37 38
Control tower 39
Red flag 40
Bureau de change
41
Trolleys 42 43 44
45 46 47 48
Person with torn
ticket 49

Cargo hold 50
Big box of
chocolates 51
Great Aunt Marigold
52

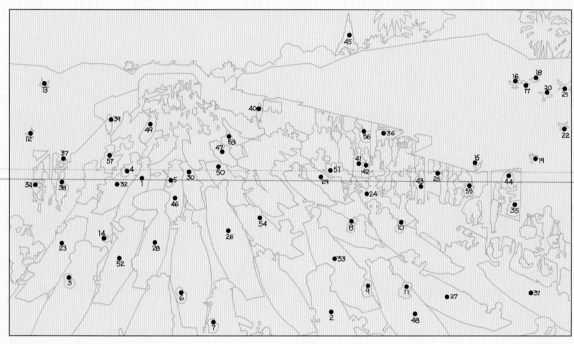

Floating market 54–55

Boats selling hats
1 2
Weighing scales 3 4
5 6 7 8 9 10 11
Purple-throated
sunbirds 12 13 14
15 16 17 18 19
20 21 22
Boats selling cooked
food 23 24
Corn on the cob
seller 25
Boats full of
watermelons 26 27
Boats full of
coconuts 28 29
Boats full of
pineapples 30 31
Boats full of limes
32 33
Wooden table 34
Embroidered
cushions 35
Silver necklaces 36
Lacquerware ducks
37
Buddhist monks 38
39 40 41 42 43
Silk jacket 44

Buddhist temple 45
Boats selling fish 46
47 48
Boats selling pots
and pans 49 50 51
Boats selling flowers
52 53 54
Dolls 55
Painted parasol 56
Great Aunt Marigold
57

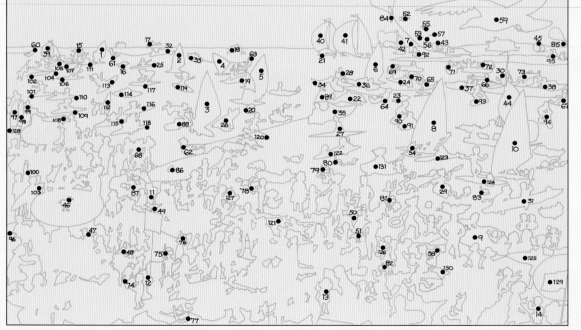

On the beach 56–57

Sailboards 1 2 3 4 5
6 7 8 9 10
People putting on
sunblock 11 12 13
14
Dolphins 15 16 17
18 19 20 21 22
23 24
Kayaks 25 26 27
28 29 30 31
Speedboats 32 33
34 35 36 37 38
Sailboats 39 40 41
42 43 44 45
Seagulls 46 47 48
49 50 51 52 53
54 55 56 57 58
59
Water-skiers 60 61
62 63 64 65 66
67
Lifesaver team 68
Divers 69 70 71 72
73
Snorkels 74 75 76
77 78 79 80 81
82 83
Parasailers 84 85
Camera 86

Jet skis 87 88 89 90
91 92 93 94 95
Surfboards 96 97
98 99 100 101
102 103 104 105
106 107 108 109
110 111 112 113
114 115 116 117
118 119 120 121
122 123 124 125
Toy koala 126
Toy kangaroo 127
Flags 128 129
Green flippers 130
Great Aunt Marigold
131

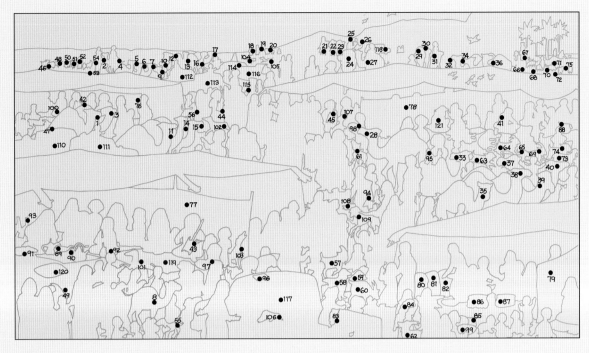

Desert homes 58–59

Camels 1 2 3 4 5 6
7 8 9 10 11 12 13
14 15 16 17 18
19 20 21 22 23
24 25 26 27 28
29 30 31 32 33
34 35 36 37 38
39 40
Person baking bread
41
Rababs 42 43 44
45
Goats 46 47 48 49
50 51 52 53 54
55 56 57 58 59
60 61 62 63 64
65 66 67 68 69
70 71 72 73 74
75
Sahahs 76 77 78 79
Sacks of dried food
80 81 82
Strings of onions 83
84 85
Metal cooking pots
86 87 88
Coffee pot 89
Ladle 90
Coffee cups 91

Pestle and mortar
92
Camel saddles 93
94 95
Book 96
Bowls of camel milk
97 98 99
Salukis 100 101
102 103 104 105
106 107 108 109
Trucks 110 111 112
113 114 115 116
117 118
Rug 119
Yellow cushion 120
Great Aunt Marigold
121

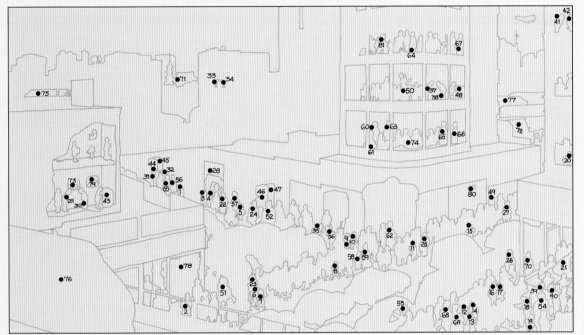

City lights 60–61

Schoolchildren 1 2
3 4 5 6 7 8 9 10
11 12 13 14 15 16
17 18 19 20
Sushi for sale 21
People wearing
masks 22 23 24 25
26 27
Chicken stall 28
People bowing 29
30 31 32 33 34
35 36 37 38 39
40 41 42
Vending machines
43 44 45 46 47
48 49
Karaoke bar 50
Sumo wrestlers 51
52 53 54
Kimonos 55 56 57
58 59 60 61 62
63 64 65 66 67
68 69 70
Temple 71
Shrine 72
Towel 73
Traditional restaurant
74

Bullet trains 75 76
77
Place selling
computers 78
Person asleep 79
Radio 80
Great Aunt Marigold
81

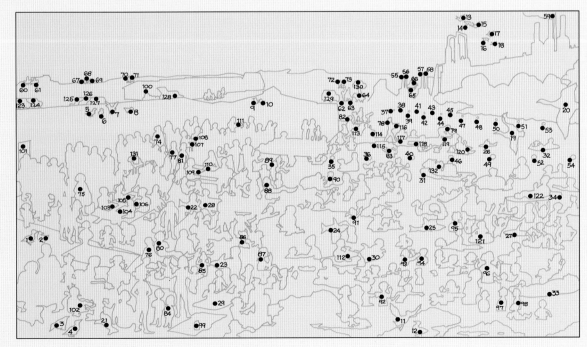

At the pool 62–63

Eider ducks 1 2 3 4
5 6 7 8 9 10 11
12 13 14 15 16 17
18 19 20
Toy sharks 21 22
23 24 25 26 27
Inflatable beds 28
29 30 31 32 33
34
Buoys 35 36 37 38
39 40 41 42 43
44 45 46 47 48
49 50 51 52 53
54
Pipes blowing out
steam 55 56 57 58
59
People horse riding
60 61 62 63 64
65 66
People hiking 67 68
69 70 71 72 73
Doctor 74
Person who has
bought face cream
75
Waiters 76 77 78
79

Waitresses 80 81
82 83
People with mud on
their faces 84 85
86 87 88 89 90
91 92 93 94 95
96 97 98
Sea-sickness pills 99
Man arriving at hotel
100
Women's changing
room 101
Food trays 102 103
104 105 106 107
108 109 110 111
112 113 114 115
116 117 118 119
120 121 122
Trucks 123 124 125
126 127 128 129
130
Bath salts 131
Great Aunt Marigold
132

91

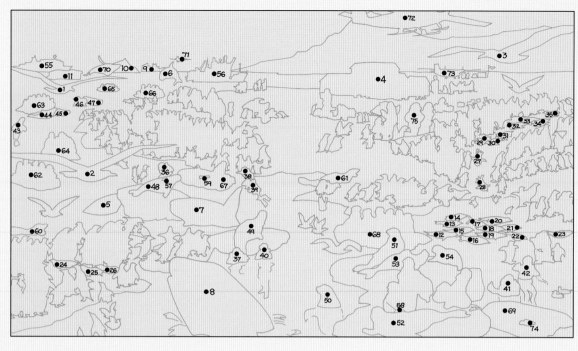

Frozen land 64–65

Albatrosses 1 2 3
Research station 4
Killer whales 5 6 7
　8
Castle iceberg 9
Pyramid iceberg 10
Greek temple
　iceberg 11
Penguins porpoising
　12 13 14 15 16 17
　18 19 20 21 22
　23
Penguins
tobogganing 24 25
　26 27 28 29 30
　31 32 33 34 35
Divers 36 37 38 39
　40 41 42
Crabeater seals 43
　44 45 46 47 48
　49 50 51 52 53
　54
Cruise ship 55
Research ship 56
Satellite tags 57 58
Flashlight 59
Leopard seals 60 61
Dinghies 62 63 64
　65 66 67 68 69

Humpback whale 70
Planes 71 72 73
Striped gloves 74
Great Aunt Marigold
　75

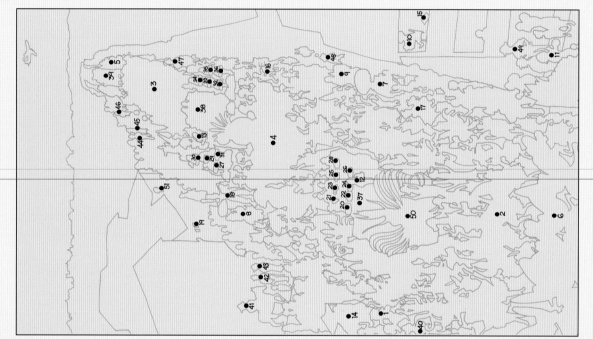

Carnival! 66–67

Great Aunt Marigold
　1
Underwater group 2
Circus group 3
Incas group 4
Spanish dancing
group 5
Flying animals group
　6
Fruit sorbet 7
Corn on the cob 8
Roti 9
Person pretending to
be a judge 10
Coconut seller 11
People singing 12 13
Fruit stall 14
Calculator 15
Jab Molassi 16
Burroquite 17
Moco Jumbie 18
Pans 19 20 21 22
　23 24 25 26 27
　28 29 30 31 32
　33 34 35 36
Floats 37 38 39
Police officers 40 41
　42 43 44 45 46
　47 48 49

Amazing costume
　50
T-shirt 51

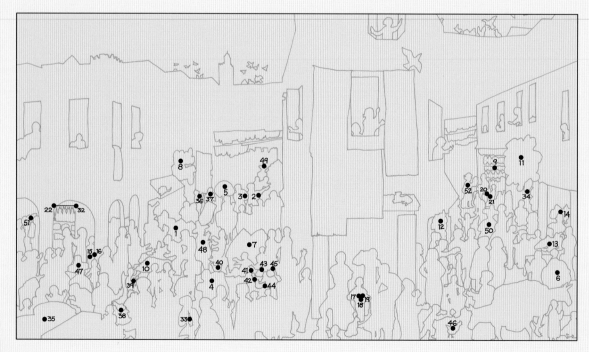

Shady souk 68–69

Herbs and spices 1
Lute 2
Drum 3
People carrying wool
　4 5 6
Dates for sale 7
Copper trays 8
Painted pottery 9
Leather slippers 10
Woven baskets 11
Embroidered caps
　12
Saddles 13 14
Glasses of mint tea
　15 16 17 18 19
　20 21
Cedarwood
containers 22 23
　24 25 26 27 28
　29 30 31 32 33
Shady hat 34
Olives 35
People bargaining
　36 37
Chickens 38 39 40
　41 42 43 44 45
　46
Water carriers 47
　48 49 50

Mirror 51
Great Aunt Marigold
　52

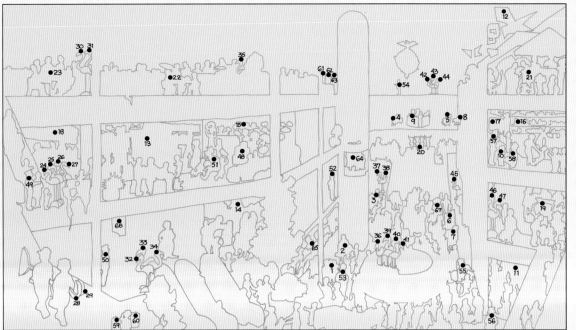

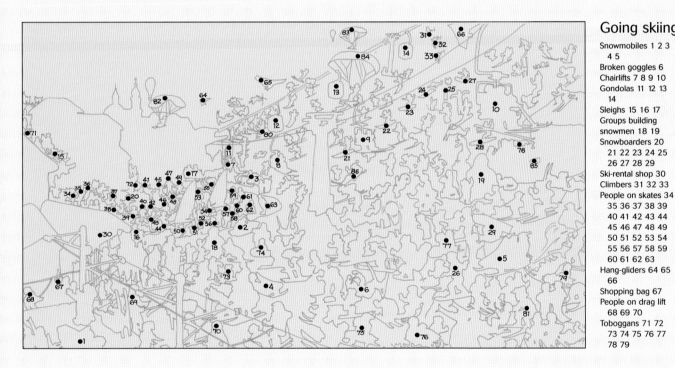

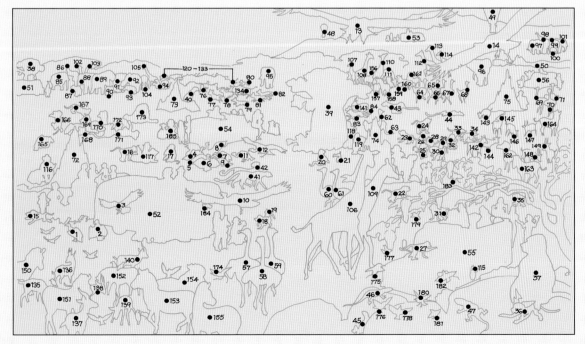

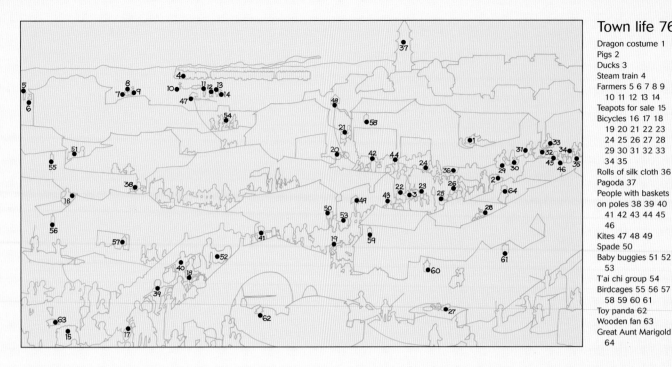

Town life 76–77

Dragon costume 1
Pigs 2
Ducks 3
Steam train 4
Farmers 5 6 7 8 9
  10 11 12 13 14
Teapots for sale 15
Bicycles 16 17 18
  19 20 21 22 23
  24 25 26 27 28
  29 30 31 32 33
  34 35
Rolls of silk cloth 36
Pagoda 37
People with baskets
on poles 38 39 40
  41 42 43 44 45
  46
Kites 47 48 49
Spade 50
Baby buggies 51 52
  53
T'ai chi group 54
Birdcages 55 56 57
  58 59 60 61
Toy panda 62
Wooden fan 63
Great Aunt Marigold
  64

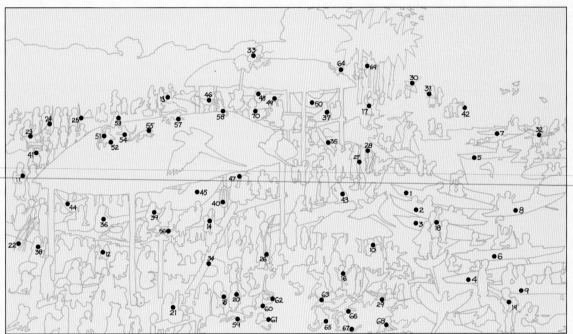

Forest people 78–79

Canoes 1 2 3 4 5 6	Red howler monkeys
7 8 9	51 52 53 54 55
Girl with anatto	56 57 58 59 60
seeds 10	61 62 63 64 65
Babies in slings 11	66 67 68
12 13 14 15 16 17	Bunch of bananas
18 19	69
Girl with parrot 20	Great Aunt Marigold
Person mashing up	70
cassava 21	
Bows 22 23 24 25	
26 27 28 29 30	
31 32	
Person mending roof	
33	
Ladders 34 35	
People weaving 36	
37	
People spinning 38	
39	
Feather garland 40	
Catapults 41 42	
Person chopping	
wood 43	
Hammocks 44 45	
46 47 48 49 50	

Island life 80–81

Donkeys 1 2 3 4 5	Windows with red
6 7 8	shutters 64 65 66
Vases 9 10 11 12 13	67 68 69 70 71
14	72 73 74
Bouzoukis 15 16 17	Mediterranean monk
18 19 20 21 22	seals 75 76
Person eating meal	Boats with oars 77
23	78 79 80 81
Churches 24 25 26	Ruins 82
Women sewing 27	Clay statue 83
28 29 30 31 32	Great Aunt Marigold
33 34 35 36	84
Necklaces 37	
Postcards 38	
Leather bags 39	
Cats 40 41 42 43	
44 45 46 47 48	
49 50 51	
Baskets of fish 52	
53 54 55	
Fishing boats 56 57	
58 59	
Tinsmith 60	
Baker 61	
Shoemaker 62	
Pad and crayons 63	

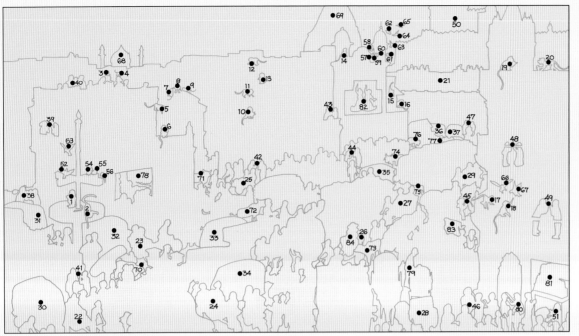

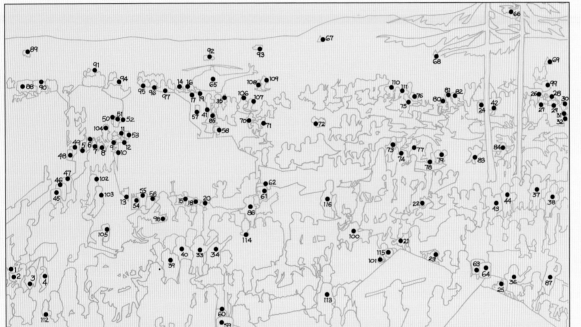

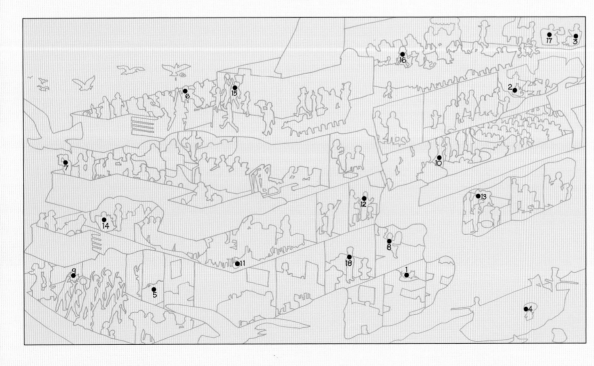

On the street 82–83

Langurs 1 2 3 4 5 6
  7 8 9 10 11 12 13
  14 15 16 17 18 19
  20
Train 21
Cycle rickshaws 22
  23 24 25 26 27
  28 29
Scooter rickshaws
  30 31 32 33 34
  35 36 37
Pairs of people
saying hello 38 39
  40 41 42 43 44
  45 46 47 48 49
Old fort 50
Tea seller 51
Crows 52 53 54 55
  56 57 58 59 60
  61 62 63 64 65
  66 67
Mosque 68
Temple 69
Cows 70 71 72 73
  74 75 76 77
Deck shoes 78
Man frying puris 79
Street barber 80
Sweetmeats 81

Cinema poster 82
Garland of flowers
  83
Great Aunt Marigold
  84

Reindeer races 84–85

Laikas 1 2 3 4 5 6
  7 8 9 10 11 12 13
  14 15 16 17 18 19
  20 21 22 23 24
  25 26 27 28 29
  30 31 32
Balalaikas 33 34 35
  36 37 38
Accordions 39 40
  41 42 43 44
Oil drums 45 46 47
  48 49 50 51 52
  53 54 55 56 57
  58 59 60 61 62
  63 64
Helicopters 65 66
Chums 67 68 69
People skating 70
  71 72 73 74 75
  76 77 78 79 80
  81 82 83 84
People chopping
wood 85 86 87
Trucks 88 89 90 91
  92 93
Snowmobiles 94 95
  96 97 98 99
Person dressing up
reindeer 100

Earmuffs 101
People on skis 102
  103 104 105
  106 107 108 109
  110 111
Toy bear 112
Person carving 113
Samovar 114
White furry hat 115
Great Aunt Marigold
  116

Cruising along 86–87

Muffin 1
Baby Nina 2
Great Aunt Eva 3
Rosie 4
Jack 5
Jo 6
Uncle Mike 7
Mrs. Choy 8
Sniff 9
Great Aunt Marigold
  10
Lennox 11
Sacha 12
The twins 13
Doctor Parekh 14
Max 15
Aunt Mimi 16
Great Uncle Frank 17
Mr. Choy 18

Test your memory

How much can you remember about the Great World Search?
Try doing this quiz to find out. The answers are on page 171.

At the airport

1. How do you get onto a plane?
   A Up a spiral staircase
   B Along a covered walkway
   C On a trolley
   D Along a yellow brick road

Floating market (Thailand)

2. Which of these is not for sale at the market?
   A Lacquerware ducks
   B Embroidered cushions
   C Dolls dressed as dancers
   D Leather shoes

On the beach (Australia)

3. Which of these might you use when swimming?
   A A snorkel
   B A snorter
   C A sneak
   D A snowflake

Desert homes (Middle East)

4. How do most Bedouin people travel today?
   A On camels
   B In trucks
   C On elephants
   D In submarines

City lights (Japan)

5. What are very fast trains in Japan called?
   A Missile trains
   B Lightning trains
   C Bullet trains
   D Tortoise trains

Frozen land (The Antarctic)

6. What do leopard seals hunt?
   A People
   B Killer whales
   C Penguins
   D Monkeys

Carnival! (Trinidad)

7. What are carnival songs in Trinidad called?
   A Carols
   B Calypsos
   C Canaries
   D Commotions

Shady souk (Morocco)

8. What is a popular drink in a Moroccan market?
   A Hot mint tea
   B Hot chocolate
   C Apple juice
   D Red wine

Going skiing (The Alps)

9. Which of these wouldn't you use to go up a slope?
   A A drag lift
   B A chairlift
   C A snowboard
   D A gondola

On safari (East Africa)

10. What is unusual about Baobab trees?
    A They live for two thousand years
    B They store lots of water in their trunks
    C They can talk in seven languages
    D They grow down instead of up

Forest people (The Amazon)

11. In the Amazon, what do Ashaninca people sleep in?
    A Holes in the ground
    B Hot-air balloons
    C Hammocks
    D Rivers

Reindeer races (Siberia)

12. What do reindeer wear while racing?
    A Earmuffs
    B Bright cloths and harnesses
    C Ice skates
    D Goggles

THE GREAT CASTLE SEARCH

Illustrated by Dominic Groebner

Contents

About the Castle Search

This part of the book is all about castles and the people who lived in them. It's also packed with challenging puzzles. The aim of each puzzle is to spot all the people, animals and objects in the scenes. If you are stuck, you can turn to pages 124 to 127 for help.

The strip at the top of the page tells you where and when the castle in the picture was built.

Around the scene are lots of little pictures.

The writing next to each little picture tells you how many of that thing you can find in the big scene.

Some little pictures are shown from a different angle than the ones in the big scene.

Some of the things you are searching for may be partly hidden, but they still count.

The story of castles

A thousand years ago, the world was a very dangerous place. Kings and lords needed somewhere safe to shelter while they fought off attacks. So they started building castles.

The castle provided a home for the lord and his family, his servants and his soldiers. It was also a place of safety for all the people who lived on the lord's land. Whenever an enemy attacked, everyone ran for cover to the castle.

Castles were often built on high ground, so soldiers could keep a lookout for enemies.

Early castles

The first castles were built around the year 900. At first, they were simply strong homes surrounded by banks of earth. But by around 1050 some people were building more complicated structures.

In England and France, kings and lords built "motte and bailey" castles. These early castles had a tall tower which stood on a mound (or motte), and a walled area known as a bailey. Most people lived in the bailey, but when an enemy attacked everyone sheltered in the tower.

Some early castles had wooden towers, but people soon started building with stone because it was much stronger.

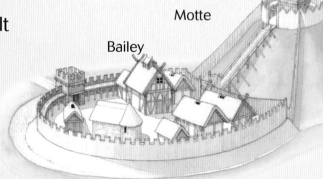

Motte

Bailey

Changing shapes

By the 1300s, armies had developed a terrifying range of weapons. So builders found new ways to make their castles stronger. They built extra walls, with walkways, watchtowers and gatehouses.

Around 1400, soldiers started blasting castle walls with cannons. People no longer felt safe in castles, and the castle as a place of refuge was on its way out.

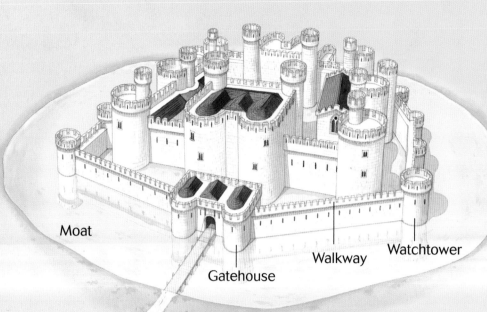

Moat

Gatehouse

Walkway

Watchtower

Heavily defended castles like this were first built by crusader knights fighting in the Middle East.

This romantic castle was built in Germany in the 1860s.

The end of the castle?

By the 1500s, most people had stopped building castles. But many rulers still wanted strong, protected homes. Samurai lords in Japan lived in tall fortresses, while Mogul emperors in India built massive forts from marble and stone.

In the 1800s, some people began to take an interest in castles again. Since then, a few wealthy individuals have built themselves "mock" castles to live in. These romantic buildings look like medieval castles, but are not intended for war.

An early castle

After the Normans conquered England in 1066, they forced the Saxon people to build castles.

Many castles had a tower on a mound, or "motte", and a walled "bailey", where the soldiers lived.

Norman soldiers were in charge. Find 17 Normans giving orders and watching the Saxons at work.

Carpenters sawed up wood. Spot six carpenters sawing wood.

The castle was protected by a palisade of wooden stakes. Find six workers building the palisade.

A winch was used to lift heavy loads. Can you see the winch?

Castle building could be very dangerous. Spot the falling Saxon.

Sometimes workers took a break. Spot 14 workers having their lunch break.

The castle was surrounded by a ditch. Find 19 Saxons with shovels working on the ditch.

Sometimes workers dropped their tools. Spot two dropped hammers.

Building materials were carried on stretchers and sleds. Find 12 stretchers and three sleds.

Some buildings had thatched roofs made from straw. Spot 17 workers laying or transporting straw.

The castle had three drawbridges. Can you find them?

Lookouts watched out for enemies. Find nine lookouts on the tower and the palisade.

Some people still worked on farms while the castle was built. Spot three farm workers.

Parts of the castle were covered in limewash. Find six builders applying limewash.

103

In the great tower

Many castles had a great tower, built from stone. The tower was the strongest part of the castle, and also the grandest. This was where the lord sometimes stayed and entertained his guests.

Merchants came to visit the lord. Find three merchants.

Tapestries helped to keep out the cold. Spot eight tapestries on the walls.

The tower had steep spiral staircases. Spot the servant falling down the steps.

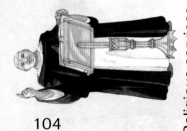

Religious services were held in the chapel. Can you see three priests?

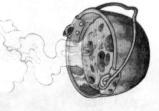

Looking out for enemies was hungry work. Find the guards having a snack.

Prisoners were captured and held in a bare room. Can you find seven prisoners?

Guards kept a lookout for signs of trouble. Find 28 guards on and off duty.

Wooden buckets were used to hold water. Spot 19 buckets of water.

The castle toilet was called the garderobe. Spot a guard on the garderobe.

There was enough food stored to last for months. Find 27 sacks of flour and 28 barrels of wine.

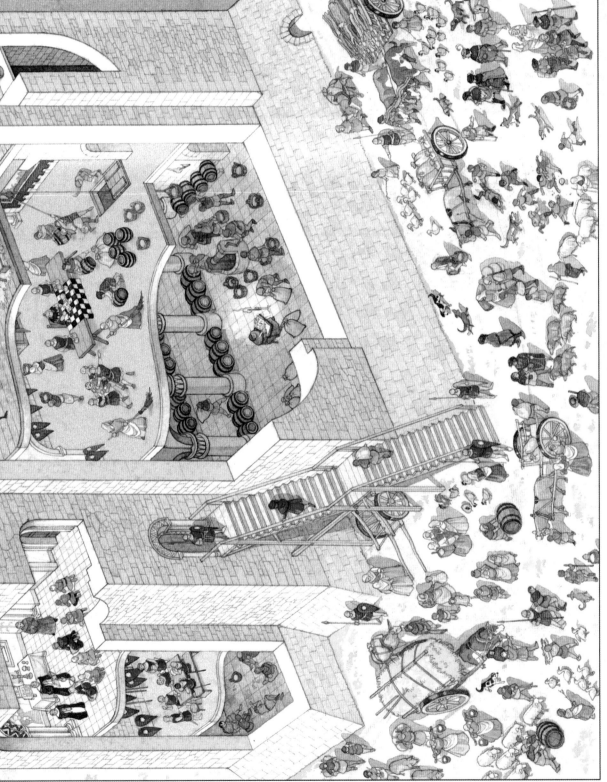

The lord held splendid feasts in the Great Hall. Find the lord seated at the high table.

The steward was in charge of the castle accounts. Spot the steward counting money.

The lord's family stayed in a room called the solar. Find the lady working on her tapestry.

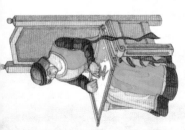

A clerk checked that none of the stores were missing. Can you see the clerk?

In the bailey

The walled area around the great tower was known as the bailey. It was full of people working hard to keep the castle running well. Most of the cooking for the castle was done in the bailey.

Carpenters made furniture and carts. Find a carpenter making a wheel.

Laundry maids spread their washing on bushes. Spot eight tunics drying on the bushes.

Cooks used large cauldrons. Can you see six cauldrons?

Carters arrived with food. Spot 10 turnips that have fallen out of this cart.

Milkmaids carried milk from the castle dairy. Find three milkmaids.

Bakers had large outdoor ovens. Find 16 loaves of bread.

Hunters brought home animals to cook. Spot two deer and eight rabbits.

Blacksmiths made and mended tools and weapons. Find 12 swords being made in the blacksmiths' forge.

Some servants had the job of sharpening knives. Can you see the three knife grinders?

The stables could get quite smelly. Spot five stable boys mucking out the stables.

Farriers made shoes for horses. Find the farrier shoeing a horse.

Children played a kind of football. Spot seven children playing with a ball.

Fletchers made wooden shafts for arrows. Find 13 arrows.

Geese were fattened up for feasts. Spot seven geese.

Under siege

During the Middle Ages, castles were often attacked by enemies, and a siege could last for months.

The attackers had some terrifying weapons, but the soldiers under siege fought back fiercely.

Trumpeters gave musical orders to the soldiers. Spot three trumpeters.

Rocks were fired from giant catapults. Find 30 rocks waiting to be fired.

Some soldiers tried to swim across the moat. Spot four swimming men.

Siege towers were wheeled close to the walls. Find 11 men in a siege tower.

Many archers used longbows. Spot 13 longbows.

Some wounded soldiers fell from the battlements. Find three falling defenders.

108

Dead animals were catapulted into the castle to spread disease. Spot the flying cow.

Knights had shields showing their family's coat of arms. Find 53 shields.

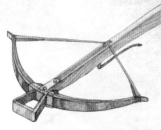

Some archers fired bolts from crossbows. Find six crossbows.

Sometimes an enemy spy sneaked into the castle in disguise. Spot the spy.

Mounted knights fought with violent weapons. Find this morning star.

Defenders dropped pots of flaming liquid. Spot four pots of fire.

Archers fired through slits in castle walls called arrow loops. Find 20 arrow loops.

Daring soldiers climbed scaling ladders. Spot six climbing or falling attackers.

At a feast

Sometimes the lord of the castle held a lavish feast in the Great Hall. Important guests sat at the high table, and merchants and knights joined in too. Feasts were very noisy and lasted for hours.

The castle cats and dogs gobbled up the scraps. Spot four cats and four dogs.

Jugglers entertained the guests. Find 11 juggling balls.

The castle servants worked very hard. Can you see six?

Cooks made elaborate dishes from marzipan. Look for the marzipan castle.

The salt container was shaped like a ship. Can you spot it?

Guests drank from gold and silver goblets. Find 31.

The lord's family emblem was displayed in many places. Try to find 10.

Stuffed swan was often served at feasts. Can you see the swan?

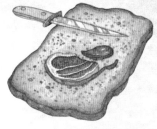

On the lower tables, people used slices of bread for plates. Spot 20.

The hall was lit by candles. Try to find nine.

Roasted boar's head was a popular dish. Can you see it?

Can you find 15 pies dropped by a clumsy page?

Tapestries hung on the walls. Spot five dogs in the tapestries.

Minstrels and entertainers performed during feasts. Find 12.

At a tournament

Tournaments were often held inside a castle's grounds. Daring knights charged at each other in mock battles, called jousts. Lords and ladies sat in decorated stands and many people joined in the fun.

A herald announced the names of the knights. Spot the herald.

Sometimes a knight wore a lady's token to show his love for her. Find two tokens.

A pie seller sold hot pies to the crowd. Can you see nine pies?

Knights jousted with long wooden poles called lances. Try to find 10.

Pages played at being knights. Find the page learning to joust.

The winning knight was given a cup. Can you spot the cup?

Can you see the page who has climbed up to get a better view?

Pickpockets roamed through the crowd. Can you see two?

Even priests came to watch the joust. Find two priests.

Knights wore splendid crests on their helmets. Spot four crests.

Wrestlers fought to see who was the strongest. Try to find four wrestlers.

Visiting knights had their own tents, called pavilions. Spot four pavilions.

Sometimes knights were wounded. Find a wounded knight.

Some people watched the joust from the castle. Spot three ladies at a balcony.

Squires helped their masters at the joust. Find seven more squires.

A family home

The lord of the castle and his family didn't live in their castle all the time, but they often stayed there. Here you can see the family in their living room, or "solar", and in the castle grounds.

The lady of the castle planned feasts with the cook. Find the cook.

Puppets were popular toys. Try to spot seven.

Boys from noble families came to be squires at the castle. Find two squires training to be knights.

Babies had silver rattles. Spot the rattle.

Girls did fine needlework. Spot three pieces of needlework.

The family owned precious handmade books, called manuscripts. Find five.

The lord and his friends went out hunting. Spot six hunting horns.

The older children played chess. Find the chess piece their little sister has taken.

Children played with spinning tops. Try to spot four.

The castle was full of dogs. Find 14 dogs inside and out.

Many people had meetings with the lord. Spot the steward and the constable.

Herbs were grown to make medicines. Spot the lord's mother in her herb garden.

The ladies used falcons to hunt for small birds. Spot six falcons.

Some children rode hobby horses. Can you find six?

A crusader castle

Crusaders were Christian knights from Europe who fought to win land around Jerusalem.

This scene shows a king and his followers visiting a castle built by crusader knights.

This castle was run by crusader knights called Hospitallers. Find 33 Hospitaller knights.

Wild animals lurked in the hills. Can you spot six wolves and a lion?

Find a lady who has fainted from heat.

The castle baker ground his flour in a windmill. Spot the windmill.

Can you see the king who has come to stay in the castle?

The crusaders kept pigeons to eat. Find 29 pigeons.

Armed knights accompanied the king. Find nine mounted knights.

Some knights were attacked and wounded on the way. Spot the wounded knight.

Squires walked beside their masters. Can you see six squires?

Mules carried sacks of food supplies. Spot five mules.

Minstrels played to the knights and ladies. Find the minstrel.

The chief guard of the castle was called the castellan. Can you spot him?

Can you spot the bishop giving thanks for a safe journey?

An aqueduct carried water to the castle. Can you see the aqueduct?

A samurai fortress

Japanese war lords lived in well-defended fortresses with their fierce samurai warriors.

In peacetime, the samurai trained for battle and the fortresses were full of life.

The lord of the fortress was called the daimyo. Can you spot him?

Nursemaids cared for the lord's children. Find three nursemaids.

Samurai warriors marched around the courtyard. Spot ten small flags on the backs of the samurai.

Laundry maids washed huge loads of clothes. Find three laundry baskets.

Young samurai learned how to fight. Find eight samurai fighting with wooden swords.

Some Buddhist priests lived in the fortress. Can you see three priests?

Merchants brought silk to show the ladies. Find three merchants bringing silk.

The lord's children loved to fly kites. Can you see five kites?

Local farmers brought food to the fortress. Find four farmers with baskets of food.

Leatherworkers made saddles for the warriors. Spot seven saddles.

Sword-makers sharpened swords on stones. Find four sword-makers.

Tall banners were fixed to the fortress walls and carried by flag-bearers. Spot nine banners.

Samurai wore breastplates made from metal strips. Spot two metalworkers making breastplates.

Poets and musicians entertained the ladies. Find a poet and two musicians.

119

A Mogul fort

The Mogul emperors of India built vast, walled forts that contained beautiful palaces, gardens and mosques. This scene shows a Mogul emperor welcoming a procession of guests to his fort.

The emperor sat on a golden throne. Spot the emperor.

There were far more men than ladies at the court. Find 19 ladies in this scene.

Some palace guards were armed with muskets. Can you see four muskets?

Musicians played many different instruments. Spot four drums, nine curved and straight horns, and two pairs of cymbals.

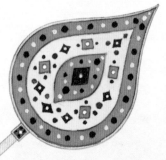

Servants waved large fans to keep the emperor cool. Find two fans.

Peacocks and monkeys roamed through the fort. Find ten peacocks and six monkeys.

Sometimes, poisonous snakes slipped into the courtyard. Spot nine snakes.

The palace artist painted pictures of important events. Spot the artist.

One mischievous monkey has stolen a turban ornament. Can you find it?

Can you see the prince who has come to visit the emperor?

The prince's courtiers carried ornaments on poles. Spot seven.

Visitors brought precious gifts for the emperor. Find four more gifts carried on cushions.

A romantic castle

Later castle-builders built "fairy-tale" homes that looked like medieval castles but were much more comfortable. This picture shows inside a romantic castle, where a party is being held.

The castle roofs were topped by fancy weathervanes. Spot five more weathervanes.

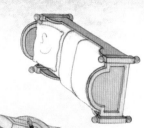

Huge banquets were prepared in the kitchen. Find the head cook.

Servants slept in small, plain rooms. Spot two servants' beds.

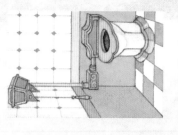

The castle had hot water for baths, and flushing toilets. Find two toilets.

Castle owners loved holding parties. Spot the king welcoming his guests.

Some guests waved to their friends arriving at the ball. Can you see 17 waving guests?

Castle owners loved to live on mountain tops. Find three other castles perched on mountains.

Musicians played romantic music. Can you see 13 musical instruments?

Some romantic castles had a "grotto" that looked like a cave. Spot the poet in his grotto.

People could lounge on comfortable sofas. Find five sofas.

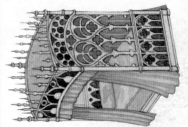

The royal bedroom was very grand. Spot the royal bed.

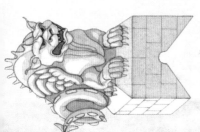

The castle had many dramatic carvings. Spot the stone dragon.

Oil paintings hung on the castle walls. Spot six oil paintings.

Food was served in beautiful dishes. Find the swan bowl.

123

Castle Search answers

The keys on the next few pages show you where to find all the people, animals and objects in the big scenes in this part of the book. You can use them to check your answers, or to help you if you have a problem finding anything.

An early castle 102–103

Norman soldiers 1	Thatchers 67 68 69
2 3 4 5 6 7 8 9	70 71 72 73 74
10 11 12 13 14 15	75 76 77 78 79
16 17	80 81 82 83

Carpenters sawing wood 18 19 20 21 22 23

Stretchers 84 85 86 87 88 89 90 91 92 93 94 95

Workers building palisade 24 25 26 27 28 29

Sleds 96 97 98

Hammers 99 100

Winch 30

Saxons with shovels 101 102 103 104 105 106 107 108 109 110 111 112 113 114 115 116 117 118 119

Falling Saxon 31

Workers on lunch break 32 33 34 35 36 37 38 39 40 41 42 43 44 45

Lookouts 46 47 48 49 50 51 52 53 54

Farm workers 55 56 57

Builders applying limewash 58 59 60 61 62 63

Drawbridges 64 65 66

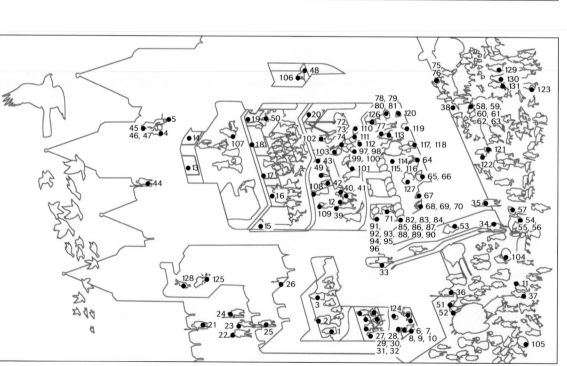

In the great tower 104–105

Priests 1 2 3

Guards sharing snack 4 5

Prisoners 6 7 8 9 10 11 12

Lady working on tapestry 13

Clerk 14

Steward 15

Lord 16

Sacks 17 18 19 20 21 22 23 24 25 26 27 28 29 30 31 32 33 34 35 36 37 38 39 40 41 42 43

Barrels 44 45 46 47 48 49 50 51 52 53 54 55 56 57 58 59 60 61 62 63 64 65 66 67 68 69 70 71

Guard on garderobe 72

Buckets 73 74 75 76 77 78 79 80 81 82 83 84 85 86 87 88 89 90 91

Guards 92 93 94 95 96 97 98 99 100 101 102 103 104 105 106 107 108 109 110 111 112 113 114 115 116 117 118 119

Falling servant 120

Tapestries 121 122 123 124 125 126 127 128

Merchants 129 130 131

In the bailey 106–107

Carpenter making wheel 1

Drying tunics 2 3 4 5 6 7 8 9

Cauldrons 10 11 12 13 14 15

Turnips 16 17 18 19 20 21 22 23 24 25

Milkmaids 26 27 28

Loaves 29 30 31 32 33 34 35 36 37 38 39 40 41 42 43 44

Children playing ball 45 46 47 48 49 50 51

Arrows 52 53 54 55 56 57 58 59 60 61 62 63 64

Geese 65 66 67 68 69 70 71

Farrier 72

Stable boys 73 74 75 76 77

Knife grinders 78 79 80

Swords 81 82 83 84 85 86 87 88 89 90 91 92

Deer 93 94

Rabbits 95 96 97 98 99 100 101 102

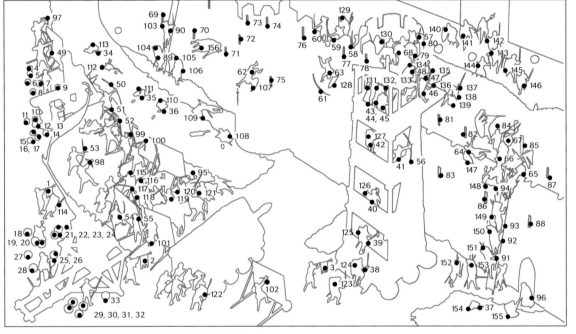

Under siege 108–109

Trumpeters 1 2 3

Rocks 4 5 6 7 8 9 10 11 12 13 14 15 16 17 18 19 20 21 22 23 24 25 26 27 28 29 30 31 32 33

Swimmers 34 35 36 37

Men in siege tower 38 39 40 41 42 43 44 45 46 47 48

Longbows 49 50 51 52 53 54 55 56 57 58 59 60 61

Falling defenders 62 63 64

Pots of fire 65 66 67 68

Arrow loops 69 70 71 72 73 74 75 76 77 78 79 80 81 82 83 84 85 86 87 88

Climbing or falling attackers 89 90 91 92 93 94

Morning star 95

Spy 96

Crossbows 97 98 99 100 101 102

Shields 103 104 105 106 107 108 109 110 111 112 113 114 115 116 117 118 119 120 121 122 123 124 125 126 127 128 129 130 131 132 133 134 135 136 137 138 139 140 141 142 143 144 145 146 147 148 149 150 151 152 153 154 155

Flying cow 156

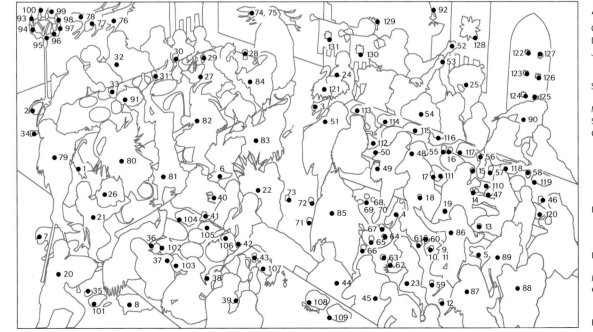

At a feast 110–111

Cats 1 2 3 4

Dogs 5 6 7 8

Juggling balls 9 10 11 12 13 14 15 16 17 18 19

Servants 20 21 22 23 24 25

Marzipan castle 26

Salt container 27

Goblets 28 29 30 31 32 33 34 35 36 37 38 39 40 41 42 43 44 45 46 47 48 49 50 51 52 53 54 55 56 57 58

Pies 59 60 61 62 63 64 65 66 67 68 69 70 71 72 73

Dogs in tapestries 74 75 76 77 78

Minstrels and entertainers 79 80 81 82 83 84 85 86 87 88 89 90

Boar's head 91

Candles 92 93 94 95 96 97 98 99 100

Bread slices 101 102 103 104 105 106 107 108 109 110 111 112 113 114 115 116 117 118 119 120

Stuffed swan 121

Family emblems 122 123 124 125 126 127 128 129 130 131

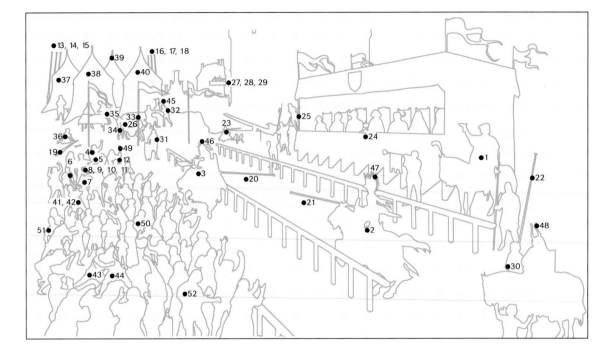

At a tournament 112–113

Herald 1
Tokens 2 3
Pies 4 5 6 7 8 9 10
  11 12
Lances 13 14 15 16
  17 18 19 20
  21 22
Jousting page 23
Cup 24
Climbing page 25
Wounded knight 26
Ladies on balcony
  27 28 29
Squires 30 31 32
  33 34 35 36
Pavilions 37 38
  39 40
Wrestlers 41 42
  43 44
Crests 45 46 47 48
Priests 49 50
Pickpockets 51 52

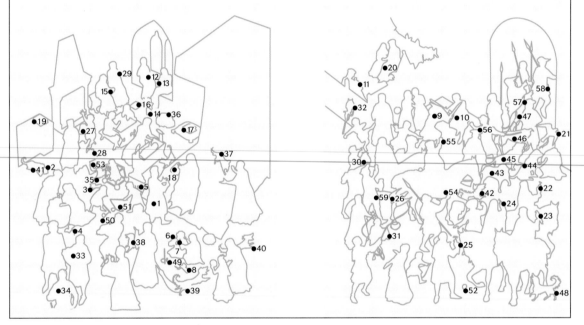

A family home 114–115

Cook 1
Puppets 2 3 4 5 6
  7 8
Squires 9 10
Rattle 11
Needlework 12
  13 14
Manuscripts 15 16
  17 18 19
Lord's mother 20
Falcons 21 22 23
  24 25 26
Hobby horses 27
  28 29 30 31 32
Steward 33
Constable 34
Dogs 35 36 37 38
  39 40 41 42 43
  44 45 46 47 48
Spinning tops 49
  50 51 52
Chess piece 53
Hunting horns 54
  55 56 57 58 59

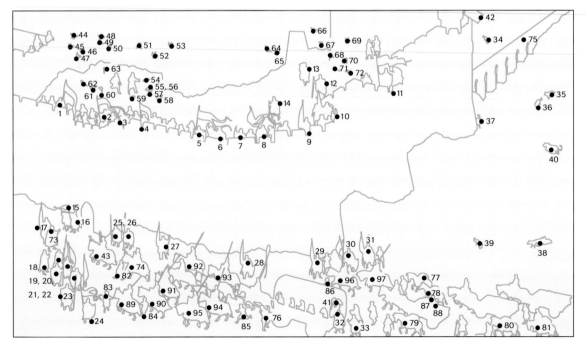

A crusader castle 116-117

Hospitaller knights
  1 2 3 4 5 6 7 8 9
  10 11 12 13 14 15
  16 17 18 19 20
  21 22 23 24 25
  26 27 28 29 30
  31 32 33
Wolves 34 35 36
  37 38 39
Lion 40
Fainting lady 41
Windmill 42
King 43
Pigeons 44 45 46
  47 48 49 50 51
  52 53 54 55 56
  57 58 59 60 61
  62 63 64 65 66
  67 68 69 70
  71 72
Castellan 73
Bishop 74
Aqueduct 75
Minstrel 76
Mules 77 78 79
  80 81

Squires 82 83 84
  85 86 87
Wounded knight 88
Mounted knights 89
  90 91 92 93 94
  95 96 97

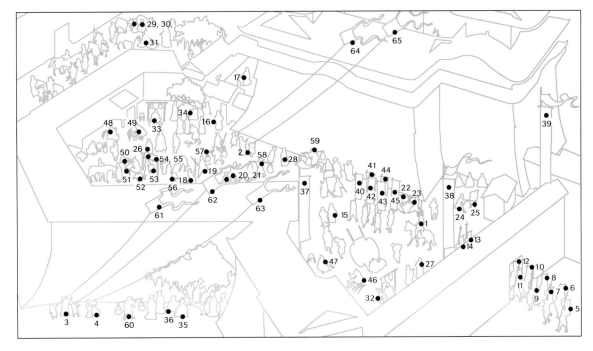

A samurai fortress 118–119

Daimyo 1
Nursemaids 2 3 4
Flags 5 6 7 8 9 10
  11 12 13 14
Laundry baskets 15
  16 17
Samurai fighting
with wooden
swords 18 19 20
  21 22 23 24 25
Priests 26 27 28
Merchants 29
  30 31
Metalworkers 32 33
Poet 34
Musicians 35 36
Banners 37 38 39
  40 41 42 43
  44 45
Sword-makers 46
  47 48 49
Saddles 50 51 52
  53 54 55 56
Farmers 57 58
  59 60
Kites 61 62 63
  64 65

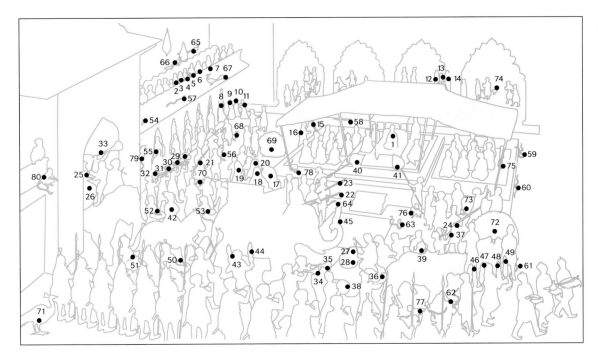

A Mogul fort 120–121

Emperor 1
Ladies 2 3 4 5 6 7
  8 9 10 11 12 13
  14 15 16 17 18
  19 20
Muskets 21 22
  23 24
Drums 25 26
  27 28
Horns 29 30 31 32
  33 34 35 36 37
Cymbals 38 39
Fans 40 41
Indian prince 42
Ornaments on poles
  43 44 45 46 47
  48 49
Gifts on cushions
  50 51 52 53
Turban ornament
  54
Artist 55
Snakes 56 57 58
  59 60 61 62
  63 64

Peacocks 65 66 67
  68 69 70 71 72
  73 74
Monkeys 75 76 77
  78 79 80

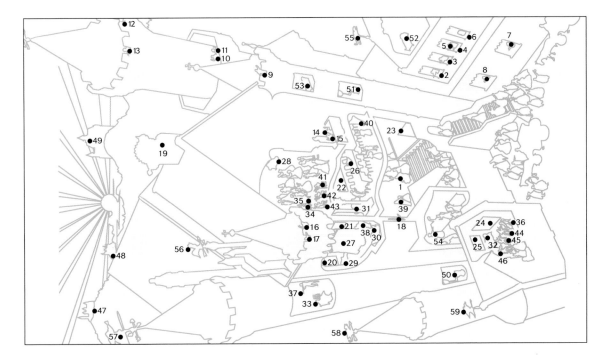

A romantic castle 122–123

King 1
Waving guests 2 3
  4 5 6 7 8 9 10 11
  12 13 14 15 16
  17 18
Stone dragon 19
Oil paintings 20 21
  22 23 24 25
Swan bowl 26
Royal bed 27
Sofas 28 29 30
  31 32
Poet 33
Cellos 34 35 36
Flute 37
Harps 38 39 40
Violins 41 42 43
  44 45 46
Castles 47 48 49
Toilets 50 51
Servants' beds
  52 53
Head cook 54
Weathervanes 55
  56 57 58 59

Test your memory

How much can you remember about the Great Castle Search?
Try doing this quiz to find out. Answers are on page 172.

An early castle
1. What was the walled area of early castles called?
   - A The bailiff
   - B The bailey
   - C The ballet
   - D The barrow

In the great tower
2. What was a castle toilet called?
   - A A wardrobe
   - B A bunker
   - C A garden
   - D A garderobe

In the bailey
3. Who made the wooden shafts for arrows?
   - A Fletchers
   - B Farriers
   - C Carpenters
   - D Minstrels

Under siege
4. Which of these wasn't used during sieges?
   - A Dead cows
   - B Rocks
   - C Flaming liquid
   - D Killer hamsters

At a feast
5. What did some people use instead of a plate?
   - A A deer skin
   - B A servant's cupped hands
   - C A slice of meat
   - D A slice of bread

At a tournament
6. Who announced the names of the knights?
   - A A harpy
   - B A herald
   - C A heron
   - D A hermit

7. What were the knights' jousting poles called?
   - A Glancers
   - B Stabbers
   - C Rapiers
   - D Lances

A family home
8. What was a family's living room called?
   - A The solar
   - B The sanctum
   - C The Great Hall
   - D The garderobe

A crusader castle
9. What were some crusader knights called?
   - A Stationers
   - B Hospitallers
   - C Wanderers
   - D Cannibals

A samurai fortress
10. What were samurai breastplates made from?
   - A Strips of wood
   - B Strips of leather
   - C Strips of metal
   - D Strips of meat

A Mogul fort
11. What did an Indian prince's courtiers carry?
   - A Bags of gold
   - B Exotic animals
   - C The prince
   - D Ornaments on poles

A romantic castle
12. What was a romantic castle's artificial cave called?
   - A The grotto
   - B The grotty
   - C The motto
   - D The maniac

THE GREAT
DINOSAUR
SEARCH

Illustrated by Studio Galante
and Inklink Firenze

Contents

About the Dinosaur Search

This part of the book is all about dinosaurs and the world they lived in. If you look hard at the pictures, you'll be able to spot hundreds of dinosaurs and the creatures that lived at the same time as them. You can see below how the puzzles in this section work.

The writing next to each little picture tells you the name of the animal or plant and how many you can find in the big picture.

Look very carefully to count all the dinosaurs in the distance.

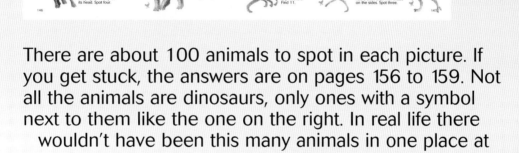

This Protoceratops is hatching, but it still counts.

These young dinosaurs also count.

Although this lizard is coming out of the big picture, you should still count it.

You can only see part of this Protoceratops, but it still counts.

There are about 100 animals to spot in each picture. If you get stuck, the answers are on pages 156 to 159. Not all the animals are dinosaurs, only ones with a symbol next to them like the one on the right. In real life there wouldn't have been this many animals in one place at the same time.

Dinosaur symbol

Shallow seas

Over 400 million years ago, the Silurian seas were full of strange creatures. Many of these have died out, but some, such as sponges and jellyfish, can still be found in the oceans today.

Heterostracan

Thelodont

Anapsid

These fish sucked food and water through their mouths. Find seven of each type.

Jellyfish looked much the same as they do now. Spot five.

Brachiopods were animals with fleshy stalks which they buried in the sand. Find 14.

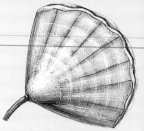

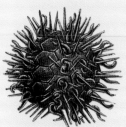

Sea urchins crawled slowly across the sea floor. Spot eight.

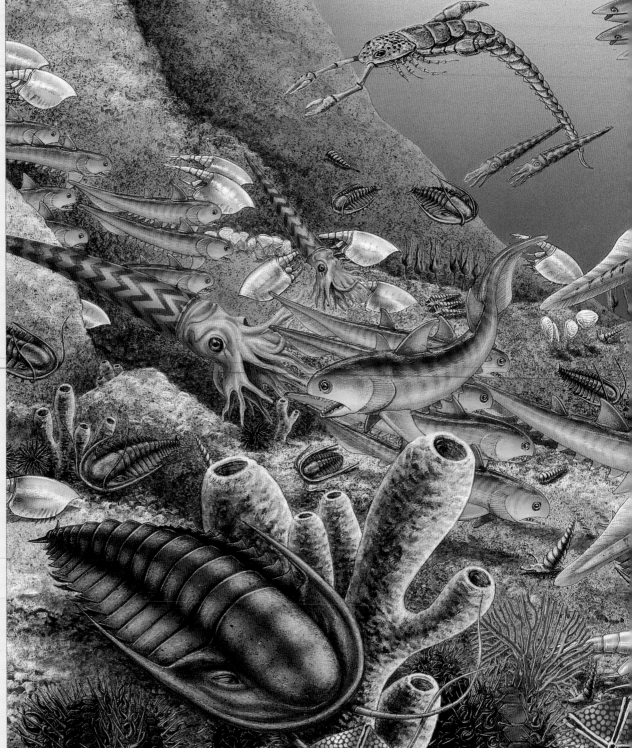

Sea-lilies were animals, not plants. They caught food with their wavy arms. Spot 15.

Marine snails could hide inside their shells. Find 14.

Nostolepis was one of the first fish to have jaws and teeth. Spot 13.

Osteostracan fish had bony shields covering their heads. Spot nine.

Cephalopods were decorated with beautiful patterns. Spot four of each of these.

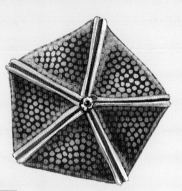

Silurian starfish didn't look the same as modern starfish. Spot 11.

Graptolites were made up of lots of small animals joined together. Find two.

Shrimps like the one above darted through the shallow water. Find 14.

Trilobites walked along the sea floor, looking for food. Spot 12.

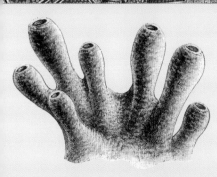

Sponges were animals with soft, fleshy bodies. Spot five.

This giant Eurypterid was a fierce hunter. Can you spot another one?

Living on the land

400 million years ago, fish with lungs for breathing air began to crawl out of the water. These fish slowly changed over millions of years, until they had legs for walking and could live on land.

Bothriolepis used its jointed fins to walk along the bottom of lakes. Spot five.

Clubmosses had branching stems covered with tiny, scaly leaves. Find nine plants.

Scientists think Aglaophyton was one of the first plants to grow on land. Spot six.

These are Ichthyostega eggs. Spot four groups.

Ichthyostega could walk on land, but it also had a fish-like tail. Spot four.

Groenlandaspis was a fish with bony plates to protect its head. Find five.

Shark-like Ctenacanthus glided through the water in search of prey. Spot one.

Ichthyostegopsis used its flipper-like legs to swim after fish. Find two.

Panderichthys had four fins that looked like arms and legs. Can you find three?

You can still see horsetail plants in wet and marshy places. Spot 16.

Water beetles looked the same as they do today. Find nine.

These woodlice were one of the first animals to live on land. Spot ten.

Shrimps fed on tiny bits of food which floated in the water. Can you find 15?

Acanthostega had gills like a fish, for breathing underwater. Spot seven.

Mimia fishes were about the size of your thumb. Spot 18.

Eusthenopteron used its fins to prop itself up on the banks of lakes and rivers. Spot three.

Giant insects

In the steamy Carboniferous swamps, gigantic insects zoomed through the air, while venomous bugs crawled through the thick, tangled undergrowth.

Pholidogaster was a strong swimmer and a fierce hunter. Spot two.

Meganeura had a wingspan that was as long as a human's arm. Spot four.

Cockroaches had flat bodies. They could squeeze under things to hide. Spot 15.

The centipede Arthropleura sometimes grew up to 2m (6fift) long. Find six.

The word Hylonomus means "forest mouse". Spot seven.

Gephyrostegus had sharp teeth for crunching up insects. Spot six.

Giant scorpions could kill other animals by stinging them. Find three.

Archaeothyris had strong jaws which helped it to kill its prey. Find three.

The first snails appeared on land at this time. Before, they had lived underwater. Spot ten.

Lizard-like microsaurs lived on land but laid their eggs in water. Spot 11.

Ophiderpeton had no arms or legs, and looked like an eel. Can you spot five?

Spiders spun simple webs to catch their prey. Find seven.

Westlothiana was a reptile. It laid eggs with hard shells and lived on dry land. Spot ten.

Giant millipedes fed on rotting leaves. Spot five.

Eogyrinus was the size of a crocodile. It snapped up fish in its powerful jaws. Find four.

Gerrothorax lay at the bottom of rivers, waiting to catch passing fish. Spot one.

137

Rocky landscape

During this time, lots of animals appeared that could live on land. The most striking of these had huge sails on their backs. Many of these creatures died out before the arrival of the dinosaurs.

Yougina had strong, sharp teeth for cracking open snail shells. Spot three.

Pareiasaurus grew as big as a hippopotamus. Spot three.

Protorosaurus reared up on its back legs to catch insects to eat. Find four.

Sphenacodon had a ridge on its back. Spot six.

Seymouria couldn't move fast on land. It spent most of its time in water. Spot three.

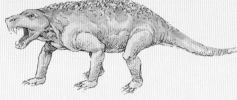

Scientists know Sauroctonus was a meat-eater, because its teeth were long and sharp. Find four.

Diadectes had legs which stuck out on either side of its body, just like a modern lizard. Spot seven.

Edaphosaurus warmed itself up by letting the Sun heat the blood in a sail on its back. Can you spot 11?

Moschops was the size of a cow. Can you find four?

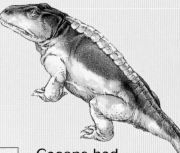

Cacops had a big head compared to the size of its body. Spot nine.

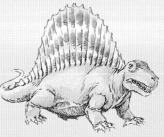

Long bones sticking out from Dimetrodon's spine held up a sail on its back. Find five.

Eryops was a distant relative of modern frogs. Spot two.

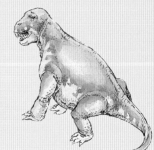

Anteosaurus bit chunks of flesh off its prey, then swallowed them whole. Spot two.

Casea had teeth all over the roof of its mouth, to crush up plants. Find four.

Scutosaurus had thick skin, and spikes sticking out of its cheeks. Spot three.

Bradysaurus had a neck frill at the back of its skull. Find one.

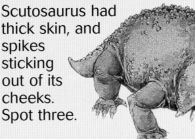

The first dinosaurs

About 225 million years ago, the first dinosaurs appeared. There are six different kinds of dinosaurs to spot here, along with some of the other strange creatures that lived at the same time.

Kuehneosaurus had thin sails of skin, which it used to glide from tree to tree. Spot four.

Although Cynognathus looked a little like a dog, it had scaly skin. Spot one.

Terrestrisuchus was about the size of a squirrel. Spot eight.

The dinosaur Staurikosaurus probably hunted in packs. Can you find seven?

The dinosaur Plateosaurus could rear up on its back legs. Find six.

Rutiodon had nostrils on the top of its head, between its eyes. Find two.

Ticinosuchus had strong, long legs so it could move very quickly. Spot five.

Saltopus, a dinosaur, scampered over rocks searching for lizards to eat. Can you find ten?

Syntarsus had sharp eyes and great speed to help it catch its prey. Spot four.

Peteinosaurus was one of the first flying lizards. Find three.

Placerias lived in herds and roamed long distances in search of food. Spot ten.

Desmatosuchus had long spikes sticking out from its shoulders. Spot three.

The dinosaur Coelophysis was a skilful hunter. Find seven.

Anchisaurus was one of the first dinosaurs. It was 2.5m (8ft) long. Spot five.

Stagonolepis may have dug for roots with its snout. Can you spot four?

Thrinaxodon had whiskers on its face and a furry body. Find five.

In the forest

The largest dinosaurs ever to walk the Earth lived at this time. Growing to enormous sizes, these giant creatures fed on the lush trees and plants which grew in the warm, wet climate.

Brachiosaurus' nostrils were on the top of a bump on its head. Spot one.

Pterodactylus snapped insects out of the air as it flew. Spot ten.

Apatosaurus swallowed leaves whole because it could not chew. Spot five.

Camptosaurus could run on its back legs if it was chased. Find two.

Fierce meat-eater Ceratosaurus had over 70 saw-edged fangs. Spot one.

Compsognathus is one of the smallest known dinosaurs. It was no bigger than a cat. Find eight.

Camarasaurus ate leaves from the lower tree branches. Spot three.

Diplodocus was as long as three buses parked end to end. Can you spot six?

Dryosaurus may have lived in herds like modern deer. Spot 17.

Archaeopteryx was probably the first bird. It flew from tree to tree. Find three.

Kentrosaurus had large spines on its back and tail. Spot one.

Scaphognathus had excellent eyesight. Can you find two?

Allosaurus had bony ridges above its eyes. Spot three.

Ornitholestes used its sharp claws to grab lizards and other small animals. Spot three.

Coelurus had long legs and could run fast to catch its prey. Spot two.

The bony plates on Stegosaurus' back may have absorbed heat from the Sun. Find two.

In the ocean

While dinosaurs roamed the land in Jurassic times, huge reptiles swam through the vast oceans.

There are 87 creatures to spot on these two pages. How many can you find?

Pleurosaurus had a long body and an even longer tail. Can you spot four?

Brittle stars still live in today's oceans. They have five long arms. Spot eight.

Plesiosaurus flapped its fins slowly up and down like a turtle. Find two.

Sharks sank to the bottom of the ocean if they didn't keep swimming. Spot six.

Liopleurodon ate other large sea creatures such as ichthyosaurs. Spot one.

Pleurosternon needed to go up to the surface to breathe. Can you spot two?

Rhomaleosaurus was as big as a modern killer whale, and just as fierce. Spot two.

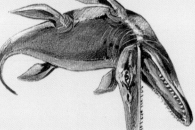

King crabs walked along the ocean floor. Spot three.

Belemnites had suckers on their arms. Spot ten.

Ichthyosaurus could swim fast by moving its powerful tail. Spot four.

Crocodile-like Geosaurus had paddle-shaped flippers. Find two.

Eurhinosaurus had a very long top jaw with lots of sharp teeth. Spot three.

Ammonites used their long tentacles to catch food. Find 14.

Teleosaurus swam with snake-like movements. Spot one.

There were many different kinds of fish. Spot ten of each of these.

Banjo fish used their wing-like fins to glide through the water. Spot five.

Dusty desert

The dinosaurs that lived in desert areas of what is now Mongolia and China suffered terrible dust storms. Some choked to death, while others were buried alive in sand dunes.

Oviraptor built nests for its eggs and sat on them until they hatched. Spot 12.

Psittacosaurus had a bony beak like a parrot's. Find four adults and six young.

Tarbosaurus ran after its prey with powerful bursts of speed. Can you find one?

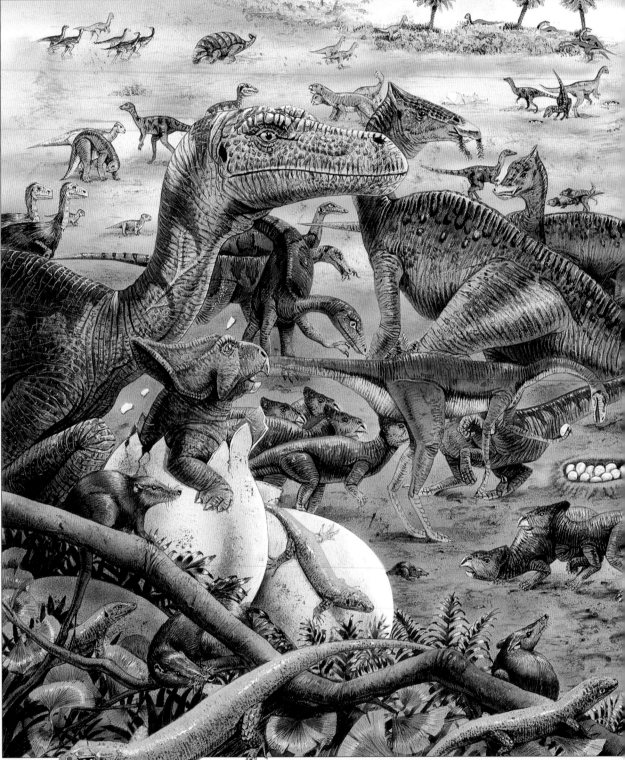

Saurolophus had a bony spike on top of its head. Spot four.

These lizards fed on dinosaur eggs. Find eight.

If Pinacosaurus was attacked, it used the club on its tail as a weapon. Spot two.

Protoceratops laid
its eggs in nests
in the sand.
Find five.

Protoceratops' nest

Microceratops
was about the
size of a rabbit.
Spot 15.

Saurornithoides
had large eyes and
may have been
able to see in the
dark. Find ten.

Small mammals
ran through the
undergrowth
catching insects
to eat. Spot five.

Bactrosaurus had
hundreds of teeth
for chewing tough
leaves. Spot seven.

Velociraptor means
"speedy killer". It
was a vicious meat-
eater. Spot six.

Gallimimus ran
on its back legs
like an ostrich,
but it didn't have
any feathers.
Find 11.

Avimimus was unusual, because it
had feathers on its body. Spot seven.

Homalocephale
had a thick skull with knobs
on the sides. Spot three.

147

The last dinosaurs

During the late Cretaceous Period, there were more types of dinosaurs than at any other point in history. But then, about 64 million years ago, the dinosaurs suddenly died out.

Parasaurolophus used a tube on its head to make trumpet-like noises. Spot six.

Styracosaurus looked very fierce, but it only ate plants. Can you spot one?

Corythosaurus had a crest-like helmet on its head. Spot three.

Edmontosaurus lived in groups for protection against predators. Spot eight.

Panoplosaurus had spikes on its sides, but its belly was unprotected. Find two.

Pachycephalosaurus males had head-butting contests. Can you find five?

Triceratops weighed twice as much as an elephant. Spot four adults and two young.

Euoplocephalus may have swung the club on the end of its tail at attackers. Find three.

Ferocious hunter Tyrannosaurus was taller than a modern giraffe. Spot one.

Stenonychosaurus may have been clever, because it had a big brain. Find seven.

Ichthyornis was one of the first birds. Find six.

Struthiomimus looked like an ostrich, but with no feathers. Spot nine.

Stegoceras belonged to a group of dinosaurs called dome heads. Spot seven.

Pentaceratops had a neck frill which reached halfway down its back. Spot three.

Nodosaurus means "lumpy reptile". Spot two.

Dromaeosaurus killed larger dinosaurs by hunting in packs. Spot 12.

Woodland mammals

When the dinosaurs died out, mammals took their place. Mammals are warm-blooded animals. They have fur or hair, give birth to babies and feed them with milk.

Tetonis gripped onto branches with its strong hands and feet. Spot five.

These bats hunted insects at night and slept during the day. Spot five.

Hyrachus was about the size of a pig. It could run very fast. Spot six.

Uintatherium was as large as a rhino, with six bony lumps on its head. Spot one.

Smilodectes used its long tail for balance as it climbed trees. Spot four.

Hyracotherium was an ancient relative of horses. Spot 11.

Coryphodon means "curved tusks". It may have used them to defend itself. Spot three.

Mesonyx had teeth like a dog, but hooves instead of paws. Find three.

Diatryma was a giant bird. It stood 2m (6fift) tall. Spot two.

Notharctus looked a little like a monkey. Spot seven.

Leptictidium was an omnivore, which means it ate plants and animals. Spot eight.

Oxyaena was a cat-like hunter that crept up on its prey. Spot two.

Venomous snakes curled around branches to sleep. Spot three.

Moeritherium probably lived in and around water. Spot one.

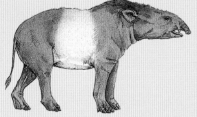

Eomanis had no teeth. It used its long tongue to lick up ants. Spot two.

Archaeotherium used its strong sense of smell to sniff out tasty roots. Spot ten.

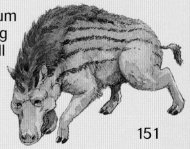

151

The Ice ages

During the Ice ages, the climate switched between very warm and extremely cold, with thick snow and ice. Here you can see some of the animals that lived in these different climates.

Columbian mammoths had tusks over 4m (13ft) long. Spot four.

Long-horned bison had poor eyesight. Can you find 12?

Woolly rhinos pushed away the snow with their horns to reach grass. Spot one.

Male cave lions were larger than lions today, but they didn't have manes. Spot one.

Like modern camels, Western camels stored water in their humps. Can you spot two?

Dire wolves used their strong teeth to crush up bones. Find six.

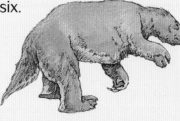

Ground sloths had bony lumps under their skin for protection. Spot one.

Teratornis swooped down to feed on dead animals. Can you find two?

Cave bears went into caves to sleep through the coldest weather. Spot two.

Grey wolves lived and hunted in packs of up to ten animals. Find seven.

Arctic hares had white fur so wolves couldn't see them against the snow. Spot seven.

Herds of ancient bison roamed the plains in search of food. Spot nine.

Reindeer had wide feet to stop them from sinking into the snow. Find ten.

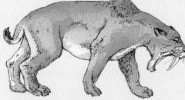
Sabre-toothed cats used their huge fangs to kill other animals. Spot two.

Woolly mammoths had very thick, shaggy fur to keep them warm. Find four.

Western horses died out 10,000 years ago, but no one knows why. Find 12.

Death of the dinosaurs

About 64 million years ago, almost all the dinosaurs died out. No one is certain why. Most scientists believe that an enormous meteorite (a rock from space) may have hit the Earth. It may have measured as much as 10km (6 miles) across.

Clouds of dust

When the meteorite hit the Earth, it would have caused a huge ball of fire to spread around the world. The meteorite would have smashed into tiny pieces, surrounding the planet with clouds of dust, rocks and water. The cloud would have blocked out all the Sun's light, making the Earth cold and dark for months.

This picture shows what may have happened as the meteorite struck the Earth.

Huge clouds of dust spread out over the Earth, making it hard for animals to breathe.

Animals dying

This would have killed any creatures that needed warmth to survive. Without light, many plants must have died as well, leaving many of the dinosaurs with nothing to eat. The meteorite may also have caused massive earthquakes and huge tidal waves.

Dinosaurs were killed or injured by pieces of flying rock.

Dinosaur puzzle

How much can you remember about the creatures you have seen in this part of the book? You may need to look back to help you with this puzzle. If you get really stuck, you'll find the answers on page 172.

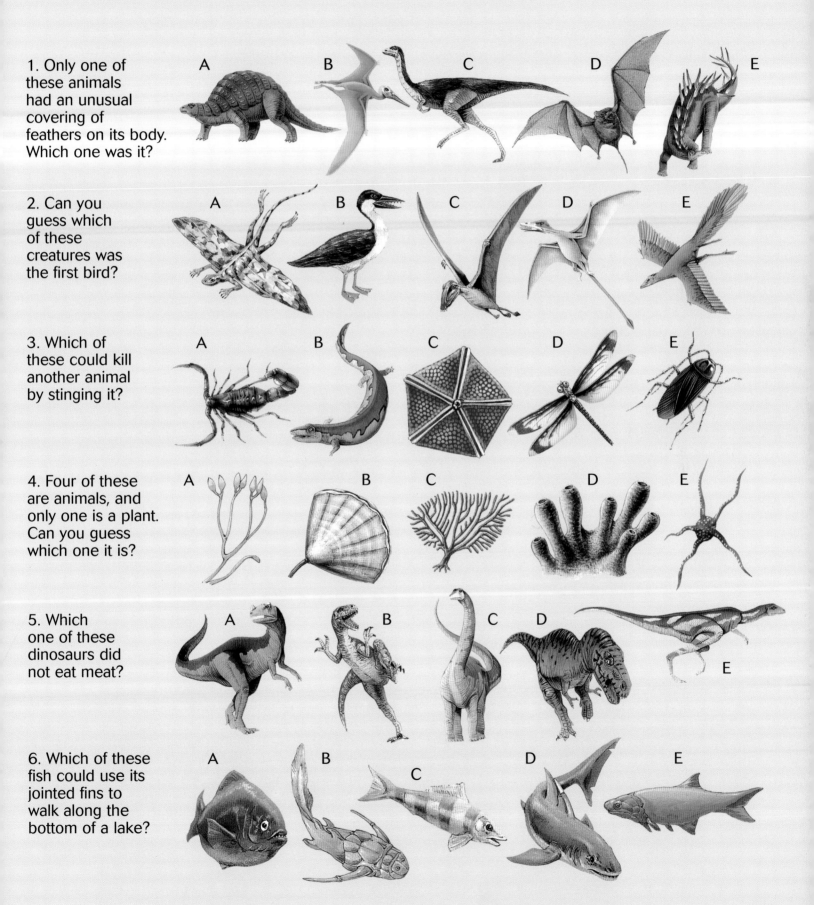

1. Only one of these animals had an unusual covering of feathers on its body. Which one was it?

A   B   C   D   E

2. Can you guess which of these creatures was the first bird?

A   B   C   D   E

3. Which of these could kill another animal by stinging it?

A   B   C   D   E

4. Four of these are animals, and only one is a plant. Can you guess which one it is?

A   B   C   D   E

5. Which one of these dinosaurs did not eat meat?

A   B   C   D   E

6. Which of these fish could use its jointed fins to walk along the bottom of a lake?

A   B   C   D   E

Quick quiz

The answers to this quick quiz are on page 172.

1. Which of these are animals?
   A Graptolite
   B Brachiopod
   C Sea urchin
   D Jellyfish

2. When did the first snails appear on land?
   A In the Silurian Period
   B In the Carboniferous Period
   C In the Permian Period
   D In the Jurassic Period

3. Which of these is not a plant-eater?
   A Camarasaurus
   B Apatosaurus
   C Ceratosaurus
   D Diplodocus

4. Which of these does not have horns?
   A Styracosaurus
   B Triceratops
   C Pentaceratops
   D Tyrannosaurus

Dinosaur Search answers

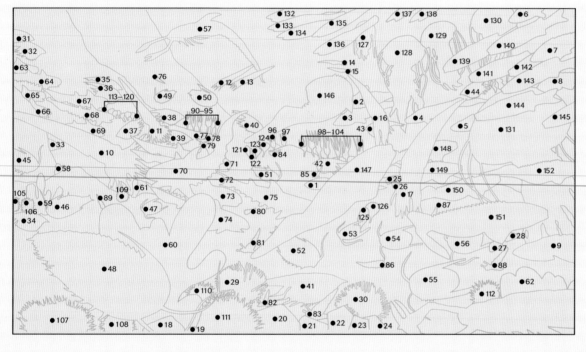

Shallow seas 132–133

Osteostracan fish
 1 2 3 4 5 6 7 8 9
Cephalopods 10 11
 12 13 14 15 16 17
Starfish 18 19 20 21
 22 23 24 25 26
 27 28
Graptolites 29 30
Shrimps 31 32 33
 34 35 36 37 38
 39 40 41 42 43
 44
Trilobites 45 46 47
 48 49 50 51 52
 53 54 55 56
Eurypterid 57
Sponges 58 59 60
 61 62
Nostolepis 63 64 65
 66 67 68 69 70
 71 72 73 74 75
Marine snails 76 77
 78 79 80 81 82
 83 84 85 86 87
 88 89
Sea-lilies 90 91 92
 93 94 95 96 97
 98 99 100 101
 102 103 104

Sea urchins 105
 106 107 108 109
 110 111 112
Brachiopods 113 114
 115 116 117 118
 119 120 121 122
 123 124 125 126
Jellyfish 127 128 129
 130 131
Heterostracan 132
 133 134 135 136
 137 138
Thelodont 139 140
 141 142 143 144
 145
Anapsid 146 147 148
 149 150 151 152

Living on the land 134–135

Ichthyostegopsis 1 2
Panderichthys 3 4 5
Horsetail plants 6 7
 8 9 10 11 12 13 14
 15 16 17 18 19
 20 21
Water beetles 22 23
 24 25 26 27 28
 29 30
Woodlice 31 32 33
 34 35 36 37 38
 39 40
Shrimps 41 42 43
 44 45 46 47 48
 49 50 51 52 53
 54 55
Eusthenopteron 56
 57 58
Mimia 59 60 61 62
 63 64 65 66 67
 68 69 70 71 72
 73 74 75 76
Acanthostega 77 78
 79 80 81 82 83
Ctenacanthus 84
Groenlandaspis 85
 86 87 88 89
Ichthyostega 90 91
 92 93

Ichthyostega's eggs
 94 95 96 97
Aglaophyton 98 99
 100 101 102 103
Clubmosses 104
 105 106 107 108
 109 110 111 112
Bothriolepis 113 114
 115 116 117

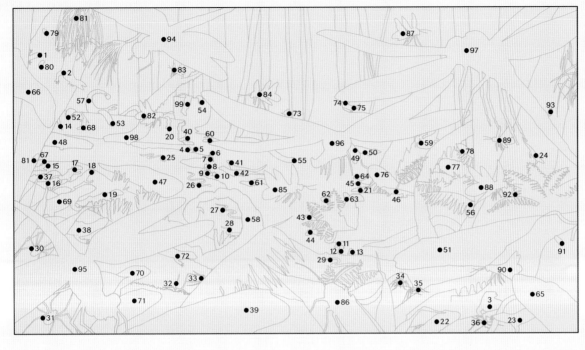

Giant insects 136–137

Archaeothyris 1 2 3
Land snails 4 5 6 7
8 9 10 11 12 13
Microsaurs 14 15 16
17 18 19 20 21
22 23 24
Ophiderpeton 25 26
27 28 29
Spiders 30 31 32
33 34 35 36
Westlothiana 37 38
39 40 41 42 43
44 45 46
Gerrothorax 47
Eogyrinus 48 49 50
51
Giant millipedes 52
53 54 55 56
Giant scorpions 57
58 59
Gephyrostegus 60
61 62 63 64 65
Hylonomus 66 67
68 69 70 71 72
Arthropleura 73 74
75 76 77 78

Cockroaches 79 80
81 82 83 84 85
86 87 88 89 90
91 92 93
Meganeura 94 95
96 97
Pholidogaster 98 99

Rocky landscape 138–139

Edaphosaurus 1 2 3
4 5 6 7 8 9 10 11
Moschops 12 13 14
15
Cacops 16 17 18 19
20 21 22 23 24
Dimetrodon 25 26
27 28 29
Eryops 30 31
Anteosaurus 32 33
Bradysaurus 34
Scutosaurus 35 36
37
Casea 38 39 40 41
Diadectes 42 43 44
45 46 47 48
Sauroctonus 49 50
51 52
Seymouria 53 54 55
Sphenacodon 56 57
58 59 60 61
Protorosaurus 62 63
64 65
Pareiasaurus 66 67
68
Yougina 69 70 71

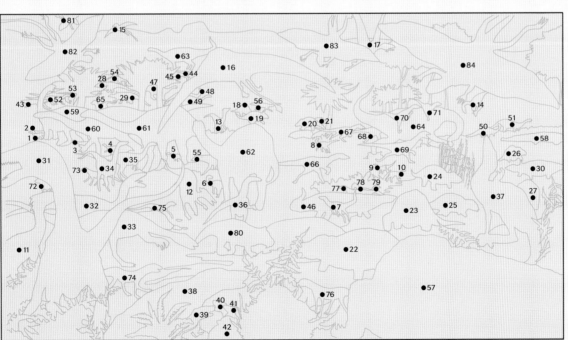

The first dinosaurs 140–141

Saltopus 1 2 3 4 5 6
7 8 9 10
Syntarsus 11 12 13
14
Peteinosaurus 15 16
17
Placerias 18 19 20
21 22 23 24 25
26 27
Desmatosuchus 28
29 30
Coelophysis 31 32
33 34 35 36 37
Thrinaxodon 38 39
40 41 42
Stagonolepis 43 44
45 46
Anchisaurus 47 48
49 50 51
Ticinosuchus 52 53
54 55 56
Rutiodon 57 58
Plateosaurus 59 60
61 62 63 64
Staurikosaurus 65
66 67 68 69 70
71

Terrestrisuchus 72
73 74 75 76 77
78 79
Cynognathus 80
Kuehneosaurus 81
82 83 84

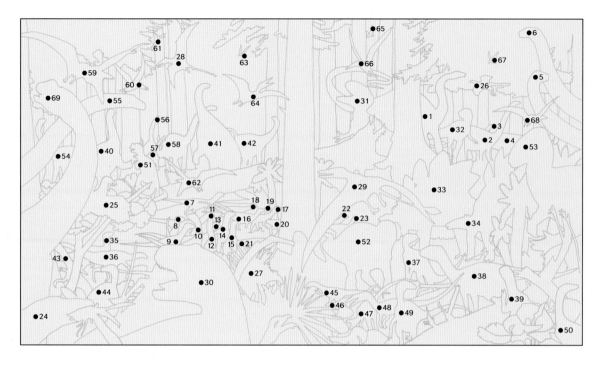

In the forest 142–143

Diplodocus 1 2 3 4
5 6
Dryosaurus 7 8 9 10
11 12 13 14 15 16
17 18 19 20 21
22 23
Archaeopteryx 24
25 26
Kentrosaurus 27
Scaphognathus 28
29
Allosaurus 30 31 32
Stegosaurus 33 34
Coelurus 35 36
Ornitholestes 37 38
39
Camarasaurus 40 41
42
Compsognathus 43
44 45 46 47 48
49 50
Ceratosaurus 51
Camptosaurus 52
53
Apatosaurus 54 55
56 57 58
Pterodactylus 59 60
61 62 63 64 65
66 67 68

Brachiosaurus 69

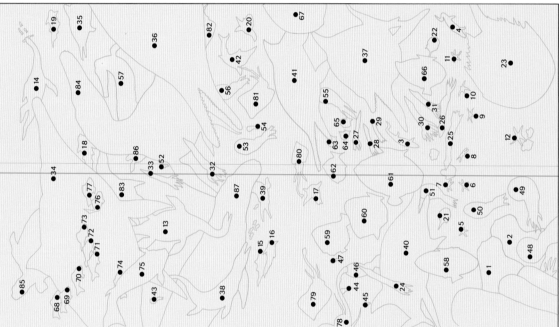

In the ocean 144–145

Pleurosaurus 1 2 3 4
Brittle stars 5 6 7 8
9 10 11 12
Plesiosaurus 13 14
Sharks 15 16 17 18
19 20
King crabs 21 22 23
Belemnites 24 25
26 27 28 29 30
31 32 33
Ichthyosaurus 34
35 36 37
Geosaurus 38 39
Eurhinosaurus 40 41
42
Ammonites 43 44
45 46 47 48 49
50 51 52 53 54
55 56
Teleosaurus 57
Fish 58 59 60 61
62 63 64 65 66
67 68 69 70 71
72 73 74 75 76
77
Banjo fish 78 79 80
81 82
Rhomaleosaurus 83
84

Pleurosternon 85 86
Liopleurodon 87

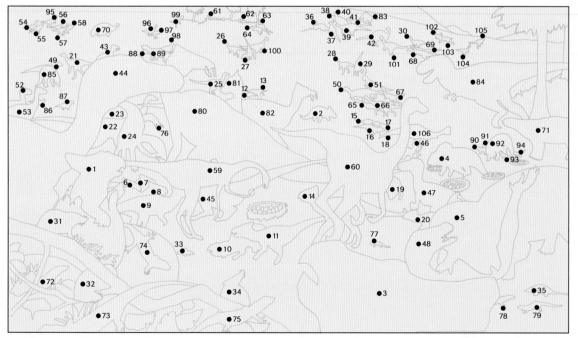

Dusty desert 146–147

Protoceratops 1 2 3
4 5
Microceratops 6 7
8 9 10 11 12 13 14
15 16 17 18 19
20
Saurornithoides 21
22 23 24 25 26
27 28 29 30
Mammals 31 32 33
34 35
Bactrosaurus 36 37
38 39 40 41 42
Velociraptor 43 44
45 46 47 48
Homalocephale 49
50 51
Avimimus 52 53 54
55 56 57 58
Gallimimus 59 60
61 62 63 64 65
66 67 68 69
Pinacosaurus 70 71
Lizards 72 73 74 75
76 77 78 79
Saurolophus 80 81
82 83
Tarbosaurus 84

Psittacosaurus 85 86
87 88 89 90 91
92 93 94
Oviraptor 95 96 97
98 99 100 101
102 103 104 105
106

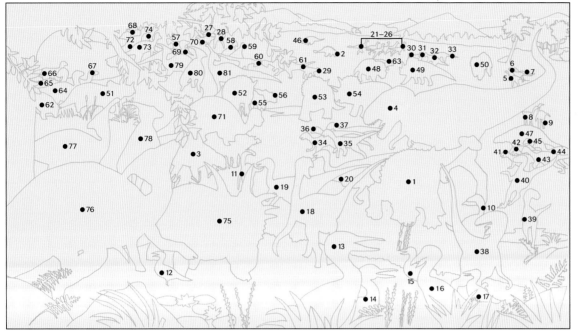

The last dinosaurs 148–149

Euoplocephalus 1 2 3
Tyrannosaurus 4
Stenonychosaurus 5 6 7 8 9 10 11
Ichthyornis 12 13 14 15 16 17
Struthiomimus 18 19 20 21 22 23 24 25 26
Stegoceras 27 28 29 30 31 32 33
Dromaeosaurus 34 35 36 37 38 39 40 41 42 43 44 45
Nodosaurus 46 47
Pentaceratops 48 49 50
Triceratops 51 52 53 54 55 56
Pachycephalosaurus 57 58 59 60 61
Panoplosaurus 62 63
Edmontosaurus 64 65 66 67 68 69 70 71

Corythosaurus 72 73 74
Styracosaurus 75
Parasaurolophus 76 77 78 79 80 81

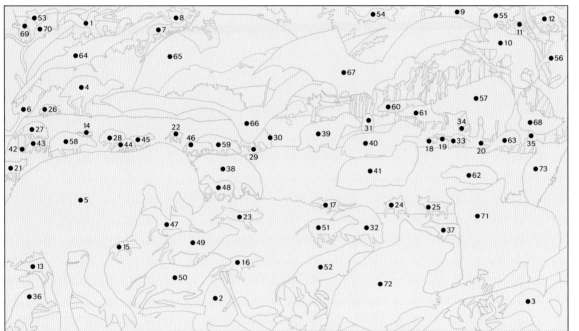

Woodland mammals 150–151

Snakes 1 2 3
Diatryma 4 5
Notharctus 6 7 8 9 10 11 12
Leptictidium 13 14 15 16 17 18 19 20
Oxyaena 21 22
Mesonyx 23 24 25
Archaeotherium 26 27 28 29 30 31 32 33 34 35
Eomanis 36 37
Moeritherium 38
Coryphodon 39 40 41
Hyracotherium 42 43 44 45 46 47 48 49 50 51 52
Smilodectes 53 54 55 56
Uintatherium 57
Hyrachus 58 59 60 61 62 63
Bats 64 65 66 67 68
Tetonis 69 70 71 72 73

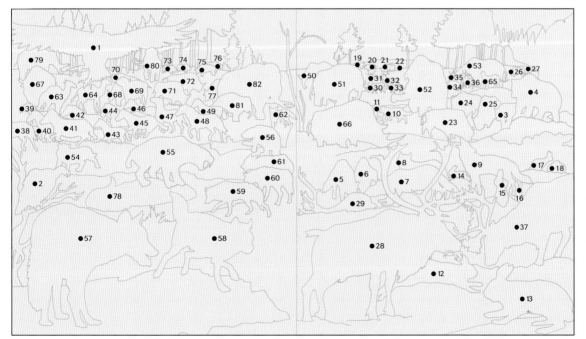

The Ice ages 152–153

Teratornis 1 2
Cave bears 3 4
Grey wolves 5 6 7 8 9 10 11
Arctic hares 12 13 14 15 16 17 18
Ancient bison 19 20 21 22 23 24 25 26 27
Reindeer 28 29 30 31 32 33 34 35 36 37
Western horses 38 39 40 41 42 43 44 45 46 47 48 49
Woolly mammoths 50 51 52 53
Sabre-toothed cats 54 55
Ground sloth 56
Dire wolves 57 58 59 60 61 62
Weatern camels 63 64
Cave lion 65
Woolly rhino 66

Long-horned bison 67 68 69 70 71 72 73 74 75 76 77 78
Columbian mammoths 79 80 81 82

Test your memory

How much can you remember about the last part of this book?
Try doing this quiz to find out. Answers are on page 172.

Shallow seas

1. What was unusual about Osteostracan fish?
   A They swam backwards
   B They had bony shields covering their heads
   C They had legs
   D They could fly

2. What were sea-lilies?
   A Plants
   B Rocks
   C Animals
   D Mermaids

Living on the land

3. Which one of these is a plant?
   A Eusthenopteron
   B Acanthostega
   C Aglaophyton
   D Groenlandaspis

4. What did Bothriolepis use its strong fins for?
   A Hitting other creatures
   B Defending itself
   C Making sand castles
   D Walking along the bottom of lakes

Giant insects

5. What does the name "Hylonomus" mean?
   A Forest mouse
   B Crazy tiger
   C Thunder lizard
   D Speedy climber

6. How long was Meganeura's wingpsan?
   A As long as a tennis court
   B As long as a human's arm
   C As long as three hundred bananas
      end to end
   D As long as a giraffe's neck

7. Where did microsaurs lay their eggs?
   A Inside holes in the ground
   B On the branches of trees
   C In the water
   D In a luminous basket in the sky

Rocky landscape

8. What was striking about some Permian animals?
   A They had two heads
   B They could change the shade of their skin
   C They could jump enormous distances
   D They had huge sails on their backs

9. Where did Seymouria spend most of its time?
   A In water
   B On the land
   C In the trees
   D Tucked up in bed with a cup
      of hot chocolate

10. What did Yougina use its sharp teeth for?
   A Smiling charmingly
   B Cracking open snail shells
   C Scratching rude messages on rocks
   D Clinging onto trees

The first dinosaurs

11. Where were Desmatosuchus's spikes?
   A On its legs
   B On its ears
   C On its shoulders
   D On its belly

12. Where were Rutiodon's nostrils?
   A On the tip of its nose
   B Between its eyes
   C On its bottom
   D On its tail

In the forest

13. How long was Diplodocus?
   A As long as a bus
   B As long as three buses parked end to end
   C As long as seven buses parked end to end
   D As long as a pencil

14. How big was Compsognathus?
   A The size of a cat
   B The size of a rat
   C The size of a cow
   D The size of a stadium

In the ocean

15. How did Plesiosaurus move through the water?
    A It flapped its big fins slowly up and down
    B It used its suckers to cling to
       another creature
    C It wriggled its long fishy tail
    D It walked along the sea floor on fifty legs

16. Why did Pleurosternon swim to the surface?
    A To see if land was nearby
    B To escape the deep-sea predators
    C To make sure the sky was still there
    D To breathe air

17. What happened to sharks if they stopped swimming?
    A They exploded
    B They sank to the bottom of the ocean
    C They turned bright yellow
    D They rose to the surface of the water

Dusty desert

18. What was Pinacosaurus's secret weapon?
    A It could breathe fire
    B It had a poisonous bite
    C It had a big bony club on its tail
    D It could terrify enemies with its piercing stare

19. What was peculiar about Psittacosaurus?
    A It had five legs
    B It had a beak like a parrot's
    C As it grew older it got smaller and smaller
    D It could sing so sweetly that its
       enemies fainted

20. What does "Velociraptor" mean?
    A Friendly helper
    B Claws of doom
    C Fire monster
    D Speedy killer

The last dinosaurs

21. What did Parasaurolophus use its tube for?
    A Drinking water
    B Digging holes
    C Attacking enemies
    D Making trumpet-like noises

22. What group of dinosaurs included Stegoceras?
    A The dome heads
    B The dumb heads
    C The metal heads
    D The red heads

Woodland mammals

23. What type of animal was Hyracotherium?
    A An early badger
    B An early horse
    C An early bird
    D An early weasel

24. How did Smilodectes use its long tail?
    A It strangled enemies with it
    B It flew around by spinning it like a helicopter
    C It tickled its friends with it
    D It used it for balance when it climbed trees

25. What do omnivores eat?
    A Plants and animals
    B Just plants
    C Just animals
    D Sweet apple pies with blueberry sauce

26. Diatryma was a giant what?
    A Cat
    B Rat
    C Bat
    D Bird

The Ice ages

27. What did prehistoric cave lions lack that modern lions have?
    A Manes
    B Claws
    C Teeth
    D Ears

28. How long ago did Western horses die out?
    A 1,000 years ago
    B 10,000 years ago
    C 100,000 years ago
    D Three weeks ago

29. Why did Arctic hares have white fur?
    A So that wolves couldn't see them in the snow
    B Because white fur is warmer than any
       other fur
    C Because it looked beautiful
    D So that they could pretend to be clouds

Death of the dinosaurs

30. According to most scientists, why did the dinosaurs die out?
    A They all fell off a cliff
    B It got too hot for them
    C A meteorite struck the Earth
    D They were hunted by a ferocious giant rabbit

True or false?

Do you know which of these facts is true, and which is false? Try making your mind up before looking back through this part of the book. The answers are on page 172.

1. A brittle star like this one can still be found in today's oceans.

7. The word Hylonomus means "forest lizard".

2. Parasaurolophus used the tube on its head to scratch its back.

8. Eryops was a distant relative of modern frogs.

3. This shark sank to the bottom of the sea if it didn't keep swimming.

9. Nodosaurus means "lumpy reptile".

4. Horsetail plants like this one still exist today.

10. Euoplocephalus used the club on its tail to stop itself from falling over.

5. Peteinosaurus was one of the first birds.

11. When the dinosaurs died out, mammals such as Tetonis took their place.

6. Mimia fishes were about the size of your thumb.

12. Moschops was the size of a bus.

Index

Answers to the extra puzzles

The answers to the puzzle on page 46 are:

1. C 2. F 3. A 4. F 5. B 6. D

The answers to the puzzle on page 47 are:

1. A 2. D 3. C 4. D 5. C 6. B

7. A 8. C 9. B 10. D 11. C 12. A

The answers to the puzzle on page 48 are:

13. B 14. D 15. C 16. D 17. D 18. C 19. C

20. D 21. A 22. D 23. C 24. A 25. B 26. D

The answers to the puzzle on page 89 are:

1. Siberia
2. East Africa
3. 8 a.m. (Thailand)
4. Airport
5. Three (The Antarctic, The Alps, Siberia)
6. Five (Middle East, Trinidad, Morocco, East Africa, Greece)
7. 18 boats; 20 planes; 8 trains; 22 buses
8. D
9. F
10. C
11. F

The answers to the puzzle on page 96 are:

1. B 2. D 3. A 4. B 5. C 6. C

7. B 8. A 9. C 10. B 11. C 12. B

The answers to the puzzle on page 128 are:

1. B	2. D	3. A	4. D	5. D	6. B
7. D	8. A	9. B	10. C	11. D	12. A

The answers to the puzzle on page 155 are:

1. C	2. E	3. A	4. A	5. C	6. B

The answers to the puzzle on page 156 are:

1. All of them   2. B   3. C   4. D

The answers to the puzzle on page 160 are:

1. B	2. C	3. C	4. D	5. A
6. B	7. C	8. D	9. A	10. B
11. C	12. B	13. B	14. A	

The answers to the puzzle on page 161 are:

15. A	16. D	17. B.	18. C	19. B	
20. D	21. D	22. A	23. B	24. D	
25. A	26. D	27. A	28. B	29. A	30. C

The answers to the puzzle on page 162 are:

1. True	2. False	3. True	4. True
5. False	6. True	7. False	8. True
9. True	10. False	11.True	12. False

Acknowledgements

The publishers would like to thank the following organizations
and individuals for their help in the preparation of this book:

Rachael Swann; Mike Olley; John Russell; Dr. David Duthie;
Natalie Abi-Ezzi; Rebecca Mills; Katarina Dragoslavić;

Mr Fred Redding, Company Archivist, Selfridges, London;
The Archive Departments at Harrods Ltd; John Lewis Partnership;
Roz Quade, BAA London Gatwick, England;
Australian Tourist Commission, London, England;
Shelagh Weir, Curator for the Middle East, Museum of Mankind
(British Museum), London, England; Ms Mitsuko Ohno;
Blue Lagoon Ltd, Grindavik, Iceland; Sheila Anderson;
Trinidad High Commissioner's Office, London, England;
David Hearns, Ski Club of Great Britain, London, England;
Frances Wood, Curator of the Chinese Collections,
British Library, London, England; The Best of Morocco;
Survival, 6 Charterhouse Buildings, London EC1N 7ET, England;
Andrew Stoddart, The Hellenic Bookservice,
91 Fortress Road, London NW5 1AG, England;
A.K. Singh, Indian Tourist Board, London, England;
Dr Alan Wood, University of Lancaster, England;
Tim Stocker, P&O Cruises, 77 New Oxford Street,
London WC1A 1PP, England.

Edited by Felicity Brooks, Jane Chisholm
and Philippa Wingate

Art Director: Mary Cartwright

Consultants:
Dr. Anne Millard
Dr. Abigail Wheatley
Dr. David Norman

Additional design: Stephanie Jones

Cover design: Francesca Allen

Additional editing:
Claire Masset and Ben Denne